ARABIC GRAMMAR UNRAVELLED

Naglaa Ghali

Fun with Arabic

Requests for permission to make copies of any part of the work should be e-mailed to Fun with Arabic, info@funwitharabic.com

Library and Archives Canada Cataloguing in Publication

Ghali, Naglaa
    Arabic grammar unravelled / Naglaa Ghali.

Includes index.
ISBN 978-0-9730512-2-3

1. Arabic language—Grammar. 2. Arabic language—Text-books
for second language learners—English speakers. I. Title.

PJ6307.G48 2008 492.782'421 C2007-905108-1

This book was printed in China

1 2 3 4 5   12 11 10 09 08

All inquiries should be addressed to
info@funwitharabic.com
http://www.funwitharabic.com

TABLE OF CONTENTS

Introduction

ARABIC GRAMMAR UNRAVELLED is an introductory course covering the fundamentals of Modern Standard Arabic grammar. With so many irregularities and rules behind vocalizations, coupled with the fact that spoken Arabic does not strictly adhere to rules of grammar, Arabic grammar can be an intimidating and difficult subject to study.

In this book, you will learn the essentials of grammar without lengthy explanation of rules. The book focuses on the language as it is used by today's speakers. It only includes rules that are key to Modern Standard Arabic, and not that of classical Arabic. It does not encompass the entire Arabic grammar; some rules are beyond the scope of this book.

The book gives a brief explanation of each topic, which provides a jumpstart for new learners of the language and a quick reference guide for advanced learners of Arabic.

The exercises and drills offered in this book are excellent practice for those who like a hands-on approach for learning the language. They are designed to be interesting and stimulating to the learner, and they aim at making you love the language. Not only will you learn the rules of Arabic grammar you will also be introduced to new vocabulary, phrases and short dialogues, which are useful for day-to-day situations.

Modern Standard Arabic is the written form of the language. It is only spoken in newscasts, public speeches, and other formal settings. Spoken Arabic varies between one Arab country and another, while written Arabic is the same throughout the Arab world. Occasionally, you will encounter different styles in writing, vocabulary, and pronunciations. Just as the English language varies between its uses of "colour" and "color" or "cookies" and "biscuits," Arabic too has various styles of writing. The differences are not profound and are understood by the majority of speakers. This book adopts the Egyptian style of writing Modern Standard Arabic.

People study Arabic for a variety of reasons. Whether for business or leisure, to discover the culture, or travel, this book tries to cater for different learners' needs. Unless you want to pursue advanced Arabic studies, don't be intimidated by the irregularities of the language. Study the rule first and keep irregularities as a reference. Set your own pace and keep on studying. After you have mastered enough Arabic, you can go back to lessons that you may have found difficult in the beginning, and try to study them again. Always remember that not all Arabic speakers adhere to all of the grammatical rules you are about to study. In this book, we will often point out rules, which are generally ignored by native speakers.

Transliteration provided in this book is intended to help you imitate the pronunciation of the Arabic words. Sounds that are unique to the Arabic language are provided using a capital letter. These usually indicate an emphatic sound, not the stress on a syllable. In general, Arabic does not have stressed syllables. Arabic also has no silent letters, all letters need to be pronounced. Rules governing vocalization of arabic are tricky to study, vowel marks are generally not written in Modern Standard Arabic. Transliteration provided in this book only includes vowel sounds that are key to pronunciation or which help explain grammatical rules.

THE ARABIC ALPHABET

ا	*alif*	long vowel aa
ب	*baa'*	b
ت	*taa'*	t
ث	*thaa'*	the letters th
ج	*geem/jeem*	g or j - *depending on the dialect*
ح	*Haa'*	emphatic H
خ	*khaa'*	kh
د	*daal*	d̦
ذ	*dhaal*	dh
ر	*raa'*	r
ز	*zaay/zayn*	z
س	*seen*	s
ش	*sheen*	sh
ص	*Saad*	emphatic S
ض	*Daad*	emphatic D
ط	*Taa'*	emphatic T
ظ	*Zaa'*	Z
ع	*ᶜayn*	no equivalent ᶜ *("A" is the closest sound)*
غ	*ghayn*	gh
ف	*faa'*	f
ق	*qaaf*	q
ك	*kaaf*	k
ل	*laam*	l
م	*meem*	m
ن	*noon*	n
ه	*haa'*	h
و	*waaw*	w, long vowel oo
ي	*yaa'*	y, long vowel ee

3

Special Marks

Vowels

In Arabic vowel sounds are represented by three vowel marks.

The *fatHa* (´) looks like a small stroke and is written above the letter. It represents the vowel "a" as in "sat".

The *kasra* (◞) looks exactly like the *fatHa* but is written below the consonant it vocalizes. It represents the short vowel "i" as in "pit."

The *Damma* (ُ) looks like a small *waaw* and is written above the letter. It represents the short vowel "u" as in "up."

Examples

Look at the Arabic letter *baa'*, for example, and notice how the pronunciation of the letter changes with its vocalization.

The letter *baa'* and a *fatHa* بَ is pronounced **ba**.

The letter *baa'* and a *kasra* بِ is pronounced **bi**.

The letter *baa'* and a *Damma* بُ is pronounced **bu**.

☾ Vowel marks can be puzzling for a new learner. In modern Arabic, these marks are rarely written and most speakers learn to pronounce the word with no vocalization. In this book, we will vocalize new words, including only important vowel marks that affect pronunciation. Vocalization is then omitted in dialogues and exercises, so you can practice reading with no vowels.

OTHER SIGNS

Some additional marks are not vowels but do affect the way a word is pronounced.

SHADDA ّ - THE DOUBLE LETTER MARK

In Arabic, if a word has a double letter, it is not written twice. Rather this is indicated by a *shadda* (ّ) on top of the consonant. When the *shadda* occurs above a consonant, that consonant is pronounced as a double letter.

To stop	*kaffa*	كَفَّ

The *shadda* on top of the *faa'* indicates that this is a double letter.

TANWEEN ً - SAY N

The *tanween* mark resembles two *fatHas* stacked on top of each other (ً). The *tanween* sounds like an "n" and usually appears over the *alif*. It can only occur at the end of a word.

Thank you	*shukran*	شُكراً

MADDA (~) - THE STRETCH MARK

The *madda* is placed above the *alif*. It usually falls at the beginning of the word. Its presence indicates a stretched *alif* or a long vowel "aa".

Miss	*aanisa*	آنِسة

5

SUKOON ○ - THE NO VOWEL MARK

The *sukoon* looks like a little circle. It is the vowelesness mark. If it occurs above a consonant, it indicates that this consonant cannot be followed by a vowel.

Yes	*na'am*	نَعْمْ

Look at this word and notice that both the *noon and the 'ayn* carry the short vowel "a." The *meem*, however, is not followed by any vowels. This is indicated by the *sukoon* mark. This sign is rarely written in modern Arabic.

HAMZA ع - THE GLOTTAL STOP

The *hamza* has no specific sound. It indicates a glottal stop. It is usually transcribed as an apostrophe and indicates a vocal break. The *hamza* is usually carried by the *alif*, the *waaw* وَ , or the *yaa'* ئ ـئـ . It can also occur alone at the end of a word; in this case the *hamza* is placed on the writing line.

Question	*su'aal*	سؤال
Tourist	*saa'iH*	سائح
Desert	*SaHaraa'*	صحراء

The *hamza* can occur above or under the *alif*. When the *hamza* occurs above the letter, (أ) the *alif* is pronounced as an "a." When the *hamza* occurs underneath, the *alif* (إ) is pronounced as an "i."

America	*amreekaa*	أمريكا
Indonesia	*indoonisiyaa*	إندونسيا

6

Taa' marbooTa ة - The feminine mark

The *taa' marbooTa* is not an alphabet letter; it is more of a feminine mark. In Arabic, all nouns are either masculine or feminine. Most, although not all, feminine nouns end with the *taa' marbooTa*.

| Pretty woman | *imra'a gameela* | امرأة جميلة |

The *taa' marbooTa* is found only at the end of a word and is pronounced as an "a." When the *taa' marbooTa* is vocalized it is pronounced as a "t."

Alif maqSoora ى - An alif or a yaa'?

Alif maqSoora can only occur at the end of a word. It represents an *alif* sound and is written like the final *yaa'* with no dots underneath.

| On | ᶜ*laa* | على |
| Ali *(a person's name)* | ᶜ*ly* | علي |

This letter could be confusing to a new learner. Often the final *yaa'* "ي," which represents the "y" or the long vowel "ee", is written with no dots. This is an element of style. In Egyptian Arabic, for example, both the *yaa'* and *alif maqSoora* are written as "ى." In order to guide you through pronunciation, in this book, we will write the final *yaa'* with two dots underneath when it represents a "y" or a long vowel "ee," and with no dots when it represents an "aa" sound. Just note that there is no conformity to this rule.

PART I

PRONOUNS

Personal Pronouns

Personal pronouns refer to specific persons or things. In English there are eight pronouns; in Arabic, there are twelve.

English	Transliteration	Arabic
I	*anaa*	أَنَا
You *(masculine, singular)*	*anta*	أَنْتَ
You *(feminine, singular)*	*anti*	أَنْتِ
He	*huwa*	هُوَ
She	*hiya*	هِيَ
We	*naHnu*	نَحْنُ
You *(dual)*	*antumaa*	أَنْتُمَا
You *(masculine, plural)*	*antum*	أَنْتُم
You *(feminine, plural)*	*antunna*	أَنْتُنَّ
They *(dual)*	*humaa*	هُمَا
They *(masculine)*	*hum*	هُمْ
They *(feminine)*	*hunna*	هُنَّ

☾ A special characteristic of Arabic is that it has personal pronouns for duals. This refers to two persons and is the same for both masculine and feminine. Another characteristic of the language is that it has a special pronoun for the second and third person feminine plural (you & they). First person singular and plural (I & we) are the same for both masculine and feminine.

☾ In spoken Arabic, the feminine plural and the dual are generally ignored. The masculine plural form is used instead of the feminine plural and also replaces the masculine and feminine duals. This also applies to informal written Arabic.

☾ The personal pronoun "It" does not exist in the Arabic language. In Arabic, all nouns are either masculine or feminine, including inanimate objects and abstracts. We will cover this in more detail in the Nouns and Adjectives section.

☾ In Arabic, the gender and number of a pronoun are usually understood from the structure of a verb. That is why personal pronouns are often omitted from a sentence. You will learn more about this when you study Verbs and Tenses.

Vocabulary

Mother	*umm*	أُمّ
Father	*ab*	أَب
Son	*ibn*	اِبن
Uncle *(maternal)*	*khaal*	خَال
Uncle *(paternal)*	*ᶜamm*	عَمّ
Brother	*akh*	أَخ
Sister	*ukht*	أُخت
Fiancé	*khaTeeb*	خَطيب
Husband	*zawg*	زَوج
Friend	*Sadeeq*	صَديق
Girl (young woman)	*fataah*	فتاة

Examples

My name is *anaa ismee*	أنا اسمى
She is pretty *hiya gameela*	هي جميلة
We are friends *naHnu aSdiqaa'*	نحن أصدقاء
Where are you (f,s) from? *min ayna anti?*	من أين أنتِ؟
You (d) are from Australia *antumaa min usturaaliyaa*	أنتما من أستراليا
You (m,s) speak Arabic *anta tataHaddathu al-ᶜarabiya*	أنت تتحدّثُ العربية
They (f) are from Lebanon *hunna min lubnaan*	هن من لبنان

GENERAL EXPRESSIONS

Yes	naʿam	نَعَم
No	laa	لاَ
Hello	ahlan	أهلاً
Hello and welcome	ahlan wa-sahlan	أهلاً وسهلاً
Here you are/Please come in	tafaDDal	تَفَضّل
Please	min faDlak	مِن فَضلك
Thank you	shukran	شُكراً
You're welcome/Pardon	ʿfwan	عفواً
Fine/O.K.	Hasanan	حَسناً
Where?	ayna	أين
From where?	min ayna	مِن أين
Beautiful	gameel	جَميل
Big	kabeer	كَبير
Small	Sagheer	صَغير
Good morning	SabaaH al-khayr	صَباح الخَير
Good morning (reply)	SabaaH an-noor	صَباح النور
Good evening	masaa' al-khayr	مَساء الخَير
God willing	in shaa' allah	إن شاء الله
Peace be with you	as-salaamu ʿalykum	السَّلامُ عَليكُم
Question particle	hal	هَل

(For questions that require yes or no answer)

Dialogue

Tarek and a group of his foreign friends meet with Mona. Follow their conversation. Take note of the exchange of greetings and the use of personal pronouns. Translation is provided in the Answers section at the end of the book.

منى: صباح الخير

Mona: SabaaH al-khayr

طارق: صباح النور. أنا طارق

Tarek: SabaaH an-noor. anaa Tarek

منى: أهلاً أنا منى. ومن هم؟

Mona: ahlaan anaa Mona. wa-man hum?

طارق: هم اصدقائي. هم لايتحدّثون العربية

Tarek: hum aSdiqaa'iee hum la yataHaddathoona al-ᶜarabiya

منى: من أين هم؟

Mona: min ayna hum?

طارق: هو من كندا وهما من أمريكا

Tarek: huwa min canadaa wa-humaa min amreekaa

منى: ومن أين أنت؟

Mona: wa-min ayna anta?

طارق: أنا من القاهرة

Tarek: anaa min al-qaahira

منى: أهلاً وسهلاً. تفضّلوا

Mona: ahlan wa-sahlan. tafaDDaloo

طارق: شكراً

Tarek: shukran

EXERCISE 1

Match these sentences with their English translation.

A. I am not from here   ١ نحن من كندا

B. We are from Canada   ٢ هم إنجليز

C. They (m) are English   ٣ هي صديقتي

D. She is my friend   ٤ أنا لست من هنا

E. You (m,s) are rich   ٥ هما متزوجان

F. They (dual) are married   ٦ أنت غني

EXERCISE 2

Solve the Puzzle.

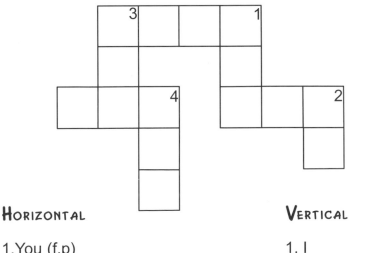

HORIZONTAL

1. You (f,p)
2. They (d)
4. You (m,s)

VERTICAL

1. I
2. She
3. We
4. You (f,s)

ATTACHED (POSSESSIVE) PRONOUNS

In Arabic, personal pronouns can also be expressed by adding pronoun suffixes. When added to a noun they indicate possession. These pronouns also serve as possessive adjectives.

☾ Let's look at the noun house or بَيت (bayt).

My house	baytee	بَيتِي
Your house (m,s)	baytuka	بَيتُكَ
Your house (f,s)	baytuki	بَيتُكِ
His house	baytuhu	بَيتُهُ
Her house	baytuhaa	بَيتُهَا
Our house	baytunaa	بَيتُنَا
Your house (m,p)	baytukum	بَيتُكُمْ
Your house (f,p)	baytukunna	بَيتُكُنَّ
Their house (m)	baytuhum	بَيتُهُمْ
Their house (f)	baytuhunna	بَيتُهُنَّ
Your house (d)	baytukumaa	بَيتُكُمَا
Their house (d)	baytuhumaa	بَيتُهُمَا

Vocabulary

Book	kitaab	كِتاب
Pen	qalam	قَلَم
Desk	maktab	مَكتَب
Car	sayyaara	سَيّارة
Bag	Haqeeba	حَقيبة
Room	ghurfa	غُرفة
School	madrasa	مَدرَسة
Family	ᶜaa'ila	عائلة

Examples

My family	ᶜaa'ilatee	عائلَتي
Our sister	ukhtunaa	أُختُنا
His paternal uncle	ᶜammuhu	عَمُّه
Our school	madrasatunaa	مَدرَسَتُنا
Their brother	akheehum	أخيهم
Your father	abeeka	أبيكَ
Their (dual) office	maktabuhumaa	مَكتَبُهُمَا

☾ Feminine nouns ending with a *taa' marbooTa* change the ending to *taa'* before adding the suffix:

مَدرَسة ← مَدرَسَتنا

☾ The dual form and the feminine plural are not commonly used in spoken Arabic.

Solve the puzzle.

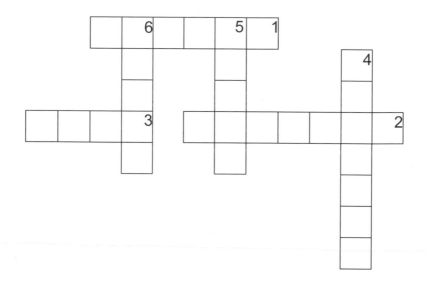

HORIZONTAL

1. Your (dual) maternal uncle

2. Their (masculine) car

3. My house

VERTICAL

4. Their (dual) friend

5. Her name

6. His office

DEMONSTRATIVE PRONOUNS

A demonstrative word is used to indicate the position of a noun in relation to the speaker. In Arabic, it takes the following forms.

This (masculine)	haadhaa	هَذَا
This (feminine)*	haadhihi	هَذِه
That (m)	dhaalika	ذَلِكَ
That (f)**	tilka	تلكَ
These dual (m)	haadhaani	هَذَانِ
These dual (f)	haataani	هَاتَانِ
These (m,f referring to people)	haa'ulaa'i	هَؤُلَاءِ
Here	hunaa	هُنَا
There	hunaak	هُنَاكَ

*هذه haadhihi is also used to refer to the plural of things that are near (equivalent to "these" in English).

This girl	haadhihi al-fataah	هذه الفتاة
These pictures	haadhihi aS-Suwar	هذه الصور

** تلك tilka is also used to indicate the plural of things that are not near (equivalent to "those" in English).

Those pictures	tilka aS-Suwar	تلك الصور

VOCABULARY

English	Transliteration	Arabic
Apartment	shaqqa	شَقَّة
House	bayt	بَيت
Garden	Hadeeqa	حَديقة
Room	ghurfa/Hugra	غُرفة/حُجرة
Kitchen	maTbakh	مَطبَخ
Hall	Saala	صالة
Living room	Saaloon	صالون
Dining room	ghurfat aT-Ta^caam	غُرفة الطَعام
Bathroom	Hammaam	حَمّام
Balcony	shurfa	شُرفة
Guest room	ghurfat aD-Duyoof	غُرفة الضيوف
Family room	ghurfat al-ma^ceesha	غُرفة المَعيشة
Big	kabeer	كَبير
Small	Sagheer	صَغير
Television	tilivisyoon	تِلفزيون
Fridge	thallaaga	ثَلاّجة
Telephone	tilyfoon/haatif	تِليفون/هاتِف
Bed	sareer	سَرير
Table	minDada	منضَدة
Dining table	sufra	سُفرة
Chair	kursee	كُرسي
Air conditioning	takyeef	تَكييف
Pictures/photos	Suwar	صُور

20

That man *dhaalika ar-ragul*	ذلك الرجل
That girl *tilka al-fataah*	تلك الفتاة
Those houses *tilka al-buyoot*	تلك البيوت
This is my father *haadhaa abee*	هذا أبي
This is my daughter *haadhihi ibnatee*	هذه اِبنتي
This is my apartment *haadhihi shaqqatee*	هذه شقّتي
These are my clothes *haadhihi malaabisee*	هذه ملابسي
These are the bride and groom *haadhaani al-ᶜaroosaan*	هذان العروسان
These (f,d) are friends *haataani Sadeeqataan*	هاتان صديقتان
These are childhood friends *haa'ulaa'i aSdiqaa' aT-Tufoola*	هؤلاء أصدقاء الطفولة
These are my nieces *haa'ulaa'i banaat akhee*	هؤلاء بنات أخي
After that *baᶜd dhaalika*	بعد ذلك
Nevertheless *maᶜa dhaalika*	مع ذلك
Here is the bedroom *hunaa ghurfat an-nawm*	هنا غرفة النوم
There is the kitchen *hunaak al-maTbakh*	هناك المطبخ

Ahmed is introducing you to his family. Place the proper demonstrative pronoun before each picture.

أخي ---
This is my brother

أخي وأختي ------
These are my brother and sister

عائلتي ---
This is my family

أصدقائي -----
These are my friends

بيتي ----
Here is my home

و--- مدرستي
and there is my school

DIALOGUE

Hala received a visit from her very curious friend Mona. Read the following dialogue and try to underline the possessive. Don't worry if there are some words you are not familiar with, you will study them in later chapters.

منى: بيتك جميل.

Mona: baytuki gameel

هالة: هذا بيتنا أنا وعائلتي.

Hala: haadhaa baytunaa anaa wa-ᶜaa'ilatee

منى: أين غرفتك؟

Mona: ayna ghurfatuki?

هالة: هذه غرفتي وهذه غرفة أخي.

Hala: haadhihi ghurfatee wa-haadhihi ghurfatu akhee

منى: غرفته كبيرة. وهل هذه صوره ؟

Mona: ghurfatuhu kabeera wa-hal haadhihi Suwaruhu?

هالة: لاهذه صور أختي هؤلاء اصدقائها.

Hala: laa haadhihi Suwaru ukhtee haa'ulaa'i aSdeeqaa'ihaa

منى: وهذه سيّارتكم؟

Mona: wa-haadhihi sayyaaratukum

هالة: نعم. هذه سيّارتنا.

Hala: naᶜam haadhihi sayyaaratunaa

Ⓒ   The conjunction letter *waaw* "و " (equivalent to "and" in English) is used to join together words or sentences. The *waaw* and the word that follows are considered one word.

VOCABULARY

Hotel	*funduq*	فُندُق
Directory	*daleel*	دَليل
Key	*miftaaH*	مِفتاح
Receptionist	*muwaZZaf al-istiqbaal*	مُوَظَّف الاستِقبال
Manager	*mudeer*	مُدير
Swimming pool	*Hammaam sibaaHa*	حَمّام سِباحة
Restaurant	*maT^cam*	مطعم
Elevator	*miS^cad*	مِصعَد

DIALOGUE

موظَّف الاستقبال: اهلاً بك في فندقنا.

muwaZZaf al-istiqbaal: ahlan bika fee funduqinaa

يوسف: شكراً. من فضلك أين المطعم؟

Youssef: shukran. min faDlaka ayna al-maT^cam?

موظَّف الاستقبال: هنا المطعم وهناك الحديقة وحمّام السباحة.

MI: hunaa al-maT^cam wa-hunaak al-Hadeeqa wa-Hammaam as-sibaaHa

يوسف: وهذه غرفتي؟

Youssef: wa-haadhihi ghurfatee?

موظَّف الاستقبال: لاهذا مكتب مدير الفندق. هذه غرفتك. تفضّل.

MI: laa haadhaa maktab mudeer al-funduq. haadhihi ghurfatuka tafaDDal

يوسف: شكراً.

Youssef: shukran

موظَّف الاستقبال: هنا غرفة النوم وهناك الحمّام. هذا دليل الفندق وهذه ثَلّاجة صغيرة. تلكَ هي الشرفة وهذان مفتاحان للغرفة. أتمنى لك إقامة طيبة.

MI: hunaa ghurfatu an-nawm wa-hunaak al-Hammaam haadhaa daleel al-funduq wa-haadhihi thallaaga Sagheera. tilka hiya ash-shurfa wa-haadhaani miftaaHaan li-lghurfa. atamanaa laka iqaama Taiyba

24

PART II

NOUNS
AND
ADJECTIVES

Nouns

A noun is a word that names a person, place, thing, idea or quality. Arabic nouns share some characteristics that may not be familiar in English.

1.   Nouns have a gender; they are masculine or feminine. Even inanimate or abstract objects have a gender.
2.   Nouns are definite or indefinite.
3.   Nouns are singular, dual, or plural.
4.   Nouns have three grammatical cases: nominative, accusative, and genitive.

Masculine and Feminine Nouns

Arabic nouns are either masculine or feminine. In Arabic, there are no neutral nouns.
Most feminine nouns follow one of the following patterns:

1. The most common form is a noun ending with a *taa' marbooTa* (ة).

Garden	*Hadeeqa*	حديقة
Library	*maktaba*	مكتبة

2. The *alif maqSoora* (ى) (see page 7).

Music	*mooseeqaa*	موسيقى

3. Most —not all—of the nouns ending with an *alif and a hamza* (اء).

Desert	*SaHaraa'*	صحراء
Sky	*samaa'*	سماء

26

4. Feminine words that, by nature, are feminine.

Mother	*umm*	أمّ
Bride	*ᶜaroos*	عروس

5. Plus a few nouns that do not fall into any of these patterns.

Sun	*shams*	شمس
Fire	*naar*	نار

VOCABULARY

The masculine noun is followed by the feminine.

Man/Woman	*ragul/imra'a*	رجل/إمرأة
Boy/Girl	*walad/bint*	ولد/بنت
Sea/Sky	*baHr/samaa'*	بحر/سماء
River/Land	*nahr/arD*	نهر/أرض
Peace/War	*salaam/Harb*	سلام/حرب
Pen/Bag	*qalam /Haqeeba*	قلم/حقيبة
Desk (office)/Room	*maktab/ghurfa*	مكتب/غرفة
House/Garden	*bayt/Hadeeqa*	بيت/حديقة
Bull/Cow	*thawr/baqara*	ثور/بقرة
Rooster/Chicken	*deek/dagaaga*	ديك/دجاجة
Married (m)/(f)	*mutazawwig/mutazawwiga*	متزوّج/متزوّجة
Engineer (m)/(f)	*muhandis/muhandisa*	مهندس/مهندسة
Moroccan (m)/(f)	*maghribee/maghribiyya*	مغربيّ/مغربيّة

Ⓒ A tip to help you out: When forming the feminine, most nouns related to people, their profession, social status and nationality are formed by adding the *taa' marbooTa* to the masculine form.

GRAMMATICAL CASES

Arabic has three grammatical cases, which are stressed in classical written Arabic but are generally ignored in Modern Standard Arabic. In spoken Arabic, case endings are only used in formal speech. Knowing the rules behind grammatical cases will help you form the plural of nouns.
The following is only a summary of the rules; a more comprehensive explanation would go beyond the scope of this book.

These three cases are:
Nominative: It is expressed by the short vowel *Damma* and is used when a noun is the subject of the sentence.
Accusative: With the *fatHa* as its case ending, it is used for the object in a sentence.
Genitive: With the *kasra* as its case ending, it is used when the noun falls after a preposition.

EXAMPLES

The teacher came   جاء المدرّسُ
gaa' al-mudarrisu

In this sentence, the teacher is the subject of the sentence so the noun takes a *Damma* as its case ending.

I saw the teacher   رأيتُ المدرّسَ
ra'aytu al-mudarrisa

In this sentence, the teacher is the object, so you add a *fatHa* to the noun.

I called the teacher   اتّصلتُ بالمدرّسِ
ittaSaltu bi-al-mudarrisi

Here, the noun is preceded by the preposition (بِ), so it takes a *kasra* as a case ending (more on prepositions page 88).

28

Definite and Indefinite Nouns

Definite Nouns

In Arabic the definite is formed by adding the prefix *alif laam* (ال) to the noun.

Examples

Man/The man	*ragul/ar-ragul*	رجل/الرَّجل
Girl/The girl	*bint/al-bint*	بنت/البنت

Sun and Moon Letters

This is not a grammatical rule, rather it is a rule governing pronunciation. Arabic letters follow two patterns in pronunciation known as the sun letters and the moon letters.

When the definite article (ال) *alif laam* joins a word starting with a sun letter, the *laam* is assimilated into the word and is not pronounced. The *laam* is pronounced when it joins a moon letter.

Examples

The moon	*al-qamar*	القمر
The sun	*ash-shams*	الشَّمس

Letters that follow the moon pattern:

ا ب ج ح خ ع غ ف ق ك م ه و ي

Letters that follow the sun pattern:

ت ث د ذ ر ز س ش ص ض ط ظ ل ن

Many Arabic speakers are ambivalent to the rules of sun and moon letters and pronounce the *laam* with sun letters. The *laam* tends to carry less stress when it is joined to a sun letter, but will not be entirely silent. You can choose to not follow this rule. After all, only a grammatical purist would notice.

INDEFINITE NOUNS

Indefinite nouns in English are preceded by the articles "a" or "an." Arabic does not have an indefinite article. Use the *tanween* mark to refer to the indefinite noun (see page 5).

The *nunation* marks are double *Damma* for indefinite nouns in the nominative (ً), double *fatHa* (ً) for the accusative, and double *kasra* for the genitive (ٍ).

Case endings for indefinite nouns in the nominative and genitive cases are usually not written. However, the case ending of the indefinite noun in the accusative case is written. This is generally formed by adding an *alif to* the indefinite noun together with the *tanween* mark.

EXAMPLES

I saw the boy	*ra'aytu al-walada*	رَأيتُ الولدَ
I saw a boy	*ra'aytu waladan*	رَأيتُ ولداً

In these examples, the noun—the boy—is in the accusative case because it is the object of the sentence. This is indicated by taking a *fatHa* as a case ending when it is definite and adding an *alif* and the *tanween* mark when it is indefinite.

☾ Not all nouns take an extra *alif* before adding the *tanween* mark. Notable exceptions are feminine nouns ending with *taa' marbooTa* or a *hamza*

EXAMPLES

I saw a cat	*ra'aytu qiTTatn*	رأيتُ قطّةً
I drove a car	*qudtu sayyaaratn*	قُدتُ سيّارةً
I loved a girl	*aHbabtu fataatn*	أحببتُ فتاةً
I bought a shoe	*ishtaraytu Hidhaa'n*	اشتريتُ حذاءً
Have a good evening	*sa'idtu masaa'n*	سعِدتُ مساءً

VOCABULARY

Here is a list of very common words in Arabic that end with the tanween mark. These are not nouns, but are important words to know.

Thank you	*shukran*	شكراً
Certainly	*Tab'an*	طبعاً
Very	*giddan*	جدّاً
Immediately	*fawran*	فوراً
Fine	*Hasanan*	حسناً
Hello	*ahlan*	اهلاً
Hello and welcome	*ahlan wa-sahlan*	اهلاً وسهلاً
Hello	*marHaban*	مرحباً
You're welcome/Pardon	*'afwan*	عفواً

PLURALS OF NOUNS

Plurals are divided into regular plurals—known as sound plurals—and irregular plurals.

REGULAR PLURALS

These are formed by adding suffixes to the noun. Masculine and feminine nouns take different suffixes.

☾ Feminine plurals are constructed by adding *alif taa'* (ات) to the singular form of the noun. A feminine noun ending with a *taa' marbooTa* drop its ending before adding the suffix.

Pretty (s/p)	*gameela/gameelaat*	جميلة/ جميلات
Artist (s/p)	*fannaana/fannaanaat*	فنّانة/ فنّانات

☾ The plural of masculine nouns is constructed by the addition of either *waaw and noon* (ون) in the nominative case, and *yaa' and noon* (ين) in the accusative and genitive cases (see page 28).

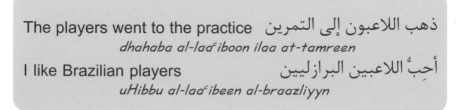

The players went to the practice ذهب اللاعبون إلى التمرين
dhahaba al-laaᶜiboon ilaa at-tamreen

I like Brazilian players أحِبُّ اللاعبين البرازليين
uHibbu al-laaᶜibeen al-braazliyyn

In the first example, the noun لاعب —a player—is the subject of the sentence so it takes the (ون) ending. In the second example, the noun is the object of the sentence so it takes the (ين) ending.

☾ Here is a tip to help you with the plurals: Many—**not all**— nouns referring to people, their social status, nationality, profession, etc., follow the regular pattern. Irregular plurals are mainly for inanimate nouns, ideas, and abstracts.

☾ Most borrowed nouns —that is, nouns which come from a foreign language—follow the pattern of the regular feminine plural.

☾ In spoken Arabic, people refer to the masculine plural by using the *yaa' noon* (ين) pattern. Only a very grammatically correct person will change the plural according to its position in the sentence. In formal written Arabic, however, proper grammatical rules must be observed.

EXAMPLES

Given below is the masculine singular followed by the feminine singular, the masculine plural (in the genitive case), and the feminine plural.

Engineer   مُهَندِس / مُهَندِسة / مُهَندِسين / مُهَندِسات
muhandis/muhandisa/muhandiseen/muhandisaat

Actor   مُمَثِّل / مُمَثِّلة / مُمَثِّلين / مُمَثِّلات
mumaththil/mumaththila/mumaththileen/mumaththilaat

Married   مُتَزَوِّج / مُتَزَوِّجة / مُتَزَوِّجين / مُتَزَوِّجات
mutazawwig/mutazawwiga/mutazawwigeen/mutazawwigaat

Saudi   سعودي / سعودية / سعوديين / سعوديّات
saᶜoudiy/saᶜoudiya/saᶜoudiyeen/saᶜoudiyyaat

Muslim   مُسلِم / مُسلِمة / مُسلِمين / مُسلِمات
muslim/muslima/muslimeen/muslimaat

C The Arabic language has many words, particularly those relating to new technology, imported from various languages. Efforts are often made to find Arabic equivalents to foreign words. Sometimes this is successful; other times the foreign word prevails. For some words, both the foreign word and its Arabic equivalent are considered correct. As more Arabic speakers are educated in foreign languages, more and more foreign words find their way into Arabic.

SOME FOREIGN WORDS

Arabic equivalents are given between brackets.

Cheque/s	شيك/شيكات
Computer/s	كمبيوتر/كمبيوترات
Television/s	تلفزيون/تلفزيونات
Sandwich/es	سندويتش/سندويتشات
Garçon (waiter)/Garçons	جرسون (نادل)/جرسونات
Democracy/Democracies	ديمقراطية/ديمقراطيات
Parliament/s	برلمان/برلمانات
Radio/s	راديو (مذياع)/راديوهات
Telephone/s	تليفون (هاتف)/تليفونات
Mobile (cell) phone/s	موبيل (محمول)/موبيلات
Coiffeur (hairdresser)/s	كوافير(مصفف شعر)/كوافيرات

IRREGULAR PLURALS

Irregular plurals do not follow a particular rule and have to be learned. There are more than a dozen patterns for the irregular plural and there is no way to tell in advance what noun follows which pattern, so you need to learn the plural with the vocabulary. The following are examples of some nouns and their plurals. Words that follow a specific pattern are grouped together. These patterns are used here only for demonstration.

PATTERN 1

Licence/Licences	*rukhSa/rukhaS*	رُخصة/رُخص
Room/Rooms	*ghurfa/ghuraf*	غُرفة/غُرَف
Picture/Pictures	*Soora/Suwar*	صورة/اصوَر

PATTERN 2

House/Houses	*bayt/buyoot*	بَيت/ابيوت
Palace/Palaces	*qaSr/quSoor*	قَصر/اقصور
Heart/Hearts	*qalb/quloob*	قَلب/اقُلوب

PATTERN 3

Rich (s/p)	*ghanee/aghniyaa'*	غَني/أغنياء
Friend/Friends	*Sadeeq/aSdiqaa'*	صَديق/أصدِقاء
Relative/Relatives	*qareeb/aqribaa'*	قَريب/أقرِباء
Smart (s/p)	*dhakee/adhkiyaa'*	ذَكي/أذكِياء

PATTERN 4

Ring/Rings	*khaatim/khawaatim*	خَاتِم/خَواتِم
Street/Streets	*shaariʿ/shawaariʿ*	شَارِع/شَوارِع

PATTERN 5

Hotel/Hotels	*funduq/fanaadiq*	فُندُق/فَنادِق
Restaurant/Restaurants	*maTʿam/maTaaʿim*	مَطعَم/مَطاعِم
Theatre/Theatres	*masraH/masaariH*	مَسرَح/مَسارِح

PATTERN 6

Week/Weeks	*usbooʿ/asaabeeʿ*	أسبوع/أسابيع
Sparrow (small bird)/s	*ʿuSfoor/ʿaSaafeer*	عُصفور/عَصافير

PATTERN 7

News (s/p)	*khabar/akhbaar*	خَبَر/أخبار
Pen/Pens	*qalam/aqlaam*	قَلَم/أقلام
Boy/Boys	*walad/awlaad*	وَلَد/أولاد
Tower/Towers	*burg/abraag*	بُرج/أبراج

PATTERN 8

Hostage/Hostages	*aseer/asraa*	أسير/أسرى
Wounded (s/p)	*gareeH/garHaa*	جَريح/جَرحى
Patient/Patients	*mareeD/marDaa*	مَريض/مَرضى

36

Magician/Magicians	saaHir/saHara	ساحِر/سَحَرة
Skilled (s/p)	maahir/mahara	ماهِر/مَهَرة
Student/Students	Taalib/Talaba	طالِب/طَلَبة (طلاب)

☾ For some nouns, the feminine plural is regular, whereas the masculine plural is not. Most of these nouns refer to people, their qualities, and their social status. Some nouns have two different masculine plural patterns. Both patterns are considered correct.

EXAMPLES

The noun in its singular masculine form is followed by the feminine singular and plural, then the masculine plural. The alternative masculine plural is given between brackets.

Single

عازِب/عازِبة/عازِبات/عزاب

ᶜaazib/ᶜaaziba/ᶜaazibaat/ᶜuzaab

Brother/Sister*

شَقيق/شَقيقة/شَقيقات/أشِقّاء (أشِقّة)

shaqeeq/shaqeeqa/shaqeeqaat/ashiqqáaʾ (ashiqqa)

Friend

صديق/صديقة/صديقات/أصدقاء

Sadeeq/Sadeeqa/Sadeeqaat/aSdiqaaʾ

Doctor

طبيب/طبيبة/طبيبات/أطبّاء

Tabeeb/Tabeeba/Tabeebaat/aTibbaaʾ

Grandparent/s

جدّ/جدّة/جدات/جدود(أجداد)

gadd/gadda/gaddaat/gudood (agdaad)

Brother/Sister*

أخ/أخت/أخوات/إخوة (إخوان)

akh/ukht/akhawaat/ikhwa (ikhwaan)

* shaqeeq is used only to stress that brothers share the same mother and father, while akh is used to refer to a brother or a half-brother.

DUALS OF NOUNS

In Arabic, to refer to two people or two things you use an ending to the word known as the dual form. Dual is formed by adding *alif* and *noon* (ا ن) in the nominative, or *yaa' noon* (ين) in the accusative and genitive cases. Feminine nouns ending with a *taa' marbooTa* change the ending to *taa'* before adding the suffix.

EXAMPLES

The bride and groom danced *raqaSa al-ᶜaroosaan*	رقص العروسان
I saw the bride and groom *ra'aytu al-ᶜaroosayn*	رأيتُ العروسين
Congratulations to the bride and groom *mabrook lil-ᶜaroosayn*	مبروك للعروسين

☾ In the first example, the noun (bride and groom) is the subject of the sentence, in the second example it is the object of the sentence, and in the third it is preceded by a preposition.

VOCABULARY

Man/Two men	*ragul/ragulaan*	رجل/رجلان
Woman/Two women	*imra'a/imra'ataan*	امرأة/امرأتان
Street/Two streets	*shaariᶜ/shaariᶜaan*	شارع/شارعان
Book/Two books	*kitaab/kitaabaan*	كتاب/كتابان
Eye/Two eyes	*ᶜayn/ᶜaynaan*	عين/عينان
Girl/Two girls	*bint/bintaan*	بنت/بنتان
Boy/Two boys	*walad/waladaan*	ولد/ولدان

VOCABULARY

In a restaurant (alternative plurals are given between brackets).

English	Transliteration	Arabic
Customer/s	zuboon/zabaa'in	زبون/زبائن
Fork/s	shawka/shuwak	شوكة/شوك
Spoon/s	miľaqa/malaaˁiq	ملعقة/ملاعق
Knife/Knives	sikkeena/sakaakeen	سكّينة/سكاكين
Plate/s	Tabaq/aTbaaq	طبق/أطباق
Glass/es	koob/akwaab	كوب/أكواب
Napkin/s	fooTa/fuwaT	فوطة/فوط
Juice/s	ˁaSeer/ˁaSaa'ir	عصير/عصائر
Egg/s	bayDa/bayD	بيضة/بيض
Meat	laHm/luHoom	لحم/الحوم
Loaf of bread/	ragheef khubz/	رغيف خبز/
Loaves of bread	arghifat khubz	أرغفة خبز
Fish/es	samaka/samak (asmaak)	سمكة/سمك (أسماك)
Chicken/s	dagaaga/dagaag	دجاجة/دجاج
Salad/s	salaTa/salaTaat	سلطة/سلطات
Dessert/s	Hulw/Halawayaat	حلو/حلويات
Vegetables	khiDar (khaDrawaat)	خضر (خضروات)
Fruit	faakiha	فاكهة
Bill/s	faatoora/fawaateer	فاتورة/فواتير
Not	ghayr	غير
To change	ghayyara	غيّر
I want	ureedu	أريد
To request	Talaba	طَلَبَ

39

DIALOGUE

Rania and her friends are having breakfast in a restaurant. The unfortunate waiter is having a hard time catering for his rather demanding customers. Follow their conversation, marking the plural and singular forms of the nouns given.

جرسون: تفضّلنَ أكواب وأطباق وفوط نظيفة.

garçon: tafaDDalna akwaab wa-aTbaaq wa-fuwaT naZeefa.

رانيا: هذا الكوب غير نظيف.

Rania: haadhaa al-koob ghayr naZeef.

هند: وهذا الطبق ايضاً غير نظيف. وأريد فوطة جديدة.

Hind: wa-haadhaa aT-Tabaq aydan ghayr naZeef wa-ureedu fooTa gadeeda.

جرسون: تفضّلنَ السكاكين والشوك.

garçon: tafaDDalna as-sakaakeen wa-ash-shuwak.

نهى: من فضلك غيّر هذه الشوكة وأريد ملعقة.

Noha: min faDlaka ghayyar haadhihi ash-shawka wa-ureedu milᶜaqa.

جرسون: سأتي لكنَّ بملاعق وعصائر طازجة.

garçon: sa-'atee la-kunna bi-malaaᶜiq wa-ᶜaSaa'ir Taaziga.

هند: أنا طلبتُ تفّاحة وليس عصير تفّاح.

Hind: anaa Talabtu tuffaaHa wa-laysa ᶜaSeer tuffaaH.

رانيا ونهى: ونحنُ طلبنا كوبين من اللبن وليس عصير.

Rania wa-Noha: wa-naHnu Talabnaa koobayn min al-laban wa-laysa ᶜaSeer.

جرسون: تفضّلنَ البيض والسندويتش وأرغفة من الخبز.

garçon: tafaDDalna al-bayD wa-as-sandweetsh wa-arghifa min al-khubz.

رانيا: ماكل هذا؟ أنا أريد رغيف وبيضة.

Rania: maa-kul haadhaa? anaa ureedu ragheef wa-bayDa.

نهى: وانا أريد سندويتشات وليس سندويتش.

Noha: wa-anaa ureedu sandweetshaat wa-laysa sandweetsh.

جرسون: تفضّلنَ الفاتورة ام تُردنَ فواتير منفصلة.

garçon: tafaDDalna al-faatoora am turidna fawaateer munfaSila.

رانيا: لا فاتورة واحدة. شكراً لك.

Rania: laa faatoora waaHida. shukran laka.

جرسون: عفواً. أنتِ زبونة جيّدة ليت كل الزبائن مثلك!

garçon: ᶜfwan. anti zuboona gayyida layta kul az-zbaa'in mithlaki.

A noun is given below with three possible answers. Can you find the right one?

1. Announcer مذيع Find the feminine plural.

I مذيعون

II مذيعين

III مذيعات

2. Accountant محاسب Find the dual of the noun.

I محاسبان

II محاسبون

III محاسبات

3. Iraqi عراقي Find the masculine plural.

I عراقيون

II عراقيات

III العراق

4. Muslim مسلم Find the dual of the noun.

I مسلمات

II مسلمون

III مسلمان

5. Parliament برلمان Find the plural.

I برلمانات

II برلمانيون

III برلمانيين

Add the plural form to the nouns below following the pattern provided.

A.	**Paper/Papers**	ورق/ أوراق
I	Light	نور ا
II	Tree	شجر II
III	Child	طفل III

B.	**War/Wars**	حرب/ حروب
I	Mind	عقل ا
II	Tiger	نمر II
III	Lion	أسد III

C.	**Camel/Camels**	جمل/ جمال
I	Mountain	جبل ا
II	Sea	بحر II
III	Wind	ريح III
IV	Arrow	سهم IV

D.	**Bag/Bags**	حقيبة/ حقائب
I	Map	خريطة ا
II	Garden	حديقة II
III	Customer	زبون III

ADJECTIVES

An adjective is a word that describes a noun. Arabic adjectives have to agree with the noun they describe in gender, number, in being definite or indefinite, and in grammatical case. In Arabic, the adjective follows the noun it refers to.

Naughty boy	walad shaqee	ولد شقي
The naughty boy	al-walad ash-shaqee	الولد الشقي
The naughty boys	al-awlaad al-ashqiyaa'	الأولاد الأشقياء

☾ One exception is the plural of an inanimate and abstract nouns, which is treated as feminine in gender.

EXAMPLES

Sweet dream	Hilm gameel	حلم جميل
Sweet dreams	aHlaam gameela	أحلام جميلة
Disturbing nightmare	kaaboos muz'ig	كابوس مزعج
Disturbing nightmares	al-kawaabees al-muz'iga	الكوابيس المزعجة
New idea	fikr gadeed	فكر جديد
New ideas	afkaar gadeeda	أفكار جديدة
Happy event	Hadath sa'eed	حدث سعيد
Happy events	aHdaath sa'eeda	أحداث سعيدة

In these examples, the adjective agrees with the noun in being definite or indefinite. However, it takes the feminine form in the plural. This only applies to the plural of inanimate and abstract nouns.

NOMINAL SENTENCE

☾ You can form nonverbal sentences (sentences with no verb, commonly referred to as nominal sentences) by using a definite noun and an indefinite adjective.

Big house	baytun kabeerun	بيتٌ كبيرٌ	I
The big house	al-baytu al-kabeeru	البيتُ الكبيرُ	II
The house is big	al-baytu kabeerun	البيتُ كبيرٌ	III

☾ In the examples above you are given a noun and adjective in their indefinite form, followed by a definite noun and adjective.

☾ In the third example, you are given a definite noun and indefinite adjective. In Arabic, this is referred to as a nominal sentence. Arabic has no equivalent to the verb "to be." The meaning is understood from the structure of the sentence. In a nominal sentence, the noun is referred to as the subject and the adjective is the predicate.

☾ In a nominal sentence, both the subject and the predicate are in the nominative case.* That is, taking a *Damma* if it is singular, an *alif noon* if it is dual, and a *waaw noon* if it is regular masculine plural.

The bride and groom are happy *al-ᶜroosaan saᶜeedaan*	العروسان سعيدان
The players are professionals *al-laaᶜiboon muHtarifoon*	اللاعبون محترفون
The girls are outstanding *al-fatayaat mutfawwqaat*	الفتيات متفوّقات

There are exceptions to this rule which will not be studied in this book.

VOCABULARY

Common Adjectives and their Opposites

New/Old	*gadeed/qadeem*	جديد/قديم
Happy/Sad	*sa'eed/Hazeen*	سعيد/حزين
Near/Far	*qareeb/ba'eed*	قريب/بعيد
Short/Long or Tall	*qaSeer/Taweel*	قصير/طويل
Poor/Rich	*ghanee/faqeer*	غني/فقير
Hot/Cold (weather)	*Haarr/baarid*	حارّ/بارد
Full/Empty	*malee'/faarigh*	ملئ/فارغ
Beautiful/Ugly	*gameel/qabeeH*	جميل/قبيح
Asleep/Awake	*naa'im/mustayqiZ*	نائم/مستيقظ
Light/Heavy	*khafeef/thaqeel*	خفيف/ثقيل
Big/Small	*kabeer/Sagheer*	كبير/صغير
Thin/Fat	*naHeef/badeen*	نحيف/بدين
Clean/Dirty	*naZeef/mutasikh*	نظيف/متسخ
Light/Dark*	*faatiH/ghaamiq*	فاتح/غامق
Light/Dark**	*muZlim/muDee'*	مظلم/مضئ
Wide/Tight or narrow	*waasi'/Dayyiq*	واسع/ضَيّق

*referring to colours, for example:

Dark dress	*fustaan ghaamiq*	فستان غامق

**referring to light, for example:

Dark room	*ghurfa muZlima*	غرفة مظلمة

Colours

Colours, in Arabic, have masculine and feminine forms. For basic colours, the feminine is formed by dropping the *alif* from the beginning of the word and adding an *alif hamza* to the end of the word. For non-basic colours, the feminine is formed by adding the *taa' marbooTa* to the end of the word.

English	Transliteration	Arabic
White	abyaD/bayDaa'	أبيض/بيضاء
Yellow	aSfar/Safraa'	أصفر/صفراء
Red	aHmar/Hamraa'	أحمر/حمراء
Green	akhDar/khaDraa'	أخضر/خضراء
Blue	azraq/zarqaa'	أزرق/زرقاء
Black	aswad/sawdaa'	أسود/سوداء
Blonde	ashqar/shaqraa'	أشقر/شقراء
Brown (brown-skinned)	asmar/samraa'	أسمر/سمراء
Brown	bunee/buniya	بني/بنية
Gold	dhahabee/dhahabiya	ذهبي/ذهبية
Silver	fiDDee/fiDDiya	فضّي/فضّية

Examples

English	Transliteration	Arabic
Blonde girl	fataah shaqraa'	فتاة شقراء
Red car	sayyaara Hamraa'	سيّارة حمراء
Silver medal	madaaliya fiDDiya	مدالية فضّية
Golden opportunity	furSa dhahabiya	فرصة ذهبية
White dress	fustaan abyaD	فستان أبيض
Green cover	ghilaaf akhDar	غلاف أخضر

VOCABULARY

Parts of the Body

Face	wagh	وَجه
Hair	sha⁣ʿr	شَعر
Head	ra´s	رأس
Eye/s (dual)	ʿayn/ʿaynaan	عَين/عينان
Ear/s (dual)	udhun/udhunaan	أذُن/أذُنان
Nose	anf	أنف
Mouth	fam	فَم
Neck	raqaba	رَقَبة
Shoulder/s (dual)	katif/katifaan	كَتف/كَتفان
Chest	Sadr	صَدر
Breast/s (dual)	thady/thadyaan	ثَدي/ثَديان
Stomach	baTn (miʿda)	بَطن (معدة)
Hand/s (dual)	yad/yadaan	يَد/يدان
Palm/s (dual)	kaff/kaffaan	كَفّ/كَفّان
Leg/s (dual)	rigl/riglaan	رِجل/رِجلان
Foot/Feet (dual)	qadam/qadamaan	قَدَم/قَدَمان
Finger/s	iSbaʿ/aSaabiʿ	إصبع/أصابِع
Body	gism	جِسم
Figure	qaama	قامة
Appearance	maZhar	مَظهَر
Muscle/s	ʿaDala/ʿaDalaat	عَضَلة/عَضَلات

47

Match the English phrase with its proper translation.

A. The new car

ا سيارة جديدة
اا سيارات جديدة
ااا السيارة الجديدة

B. Pretty eyes (dual)

ا عين جميلة
اا عيون جميلة
ااا عينان جميلتان

C. Happy dreams

ا احلام سعيد
اا احلام سعيدة
ااا احلام سعداء

D. Good news

ا أخبار سارة
اا خبر سار
ااا خبران ساران

EXERCISE 2

Place the adjective within brackets in the correct form.

ا   The handsome man   ا   الرجل (وسيم)
اا Black bag   اا حقيبة (أسود)
ااا The just peace   ااا السلام (عادل)
ااٍٍٍٍٍٍٍٍٍٍٍٍٍٍٍٍٍٍٍٍٍٍٍٍٍٍٍٍٍٍٍٍٍٍٍٍٍ

IV New ideas   IV أفكار (جديد)
V   Good story   V   قصة (جيد)
VI The naught child (f)   VI الطفلة (شقي)

ADVERTISEMENT

A director is casting for a new movie. Read the ad and underline the adjectives. Note how the adjective follows its noun.

إعلان

مخرج مشهور يبحث عن ممثلين موهوبين
المواصفات المطلوبة:

The cheating husband:	الزوج الخائن:
Black hair	شعر أسود
Tall figure	قامة طويلة
Strong muscles	عضلات قوية
Attractive eyes	عينان جذابتان

The neglected wife:	الزوجة المهملة:
Short figure	قامة قصيرة
Fat body	جسم بدين
Loud voice	صوت عال
Narrow eyes	عينان ضيقتان

The beautiful lover:	العشيقة الجميلة:
Slender body	قامة رشيقة
Blonde hair	شعر أشقر
Wide eyes	عينان واسعتان
Soft voice	صوت ناعم

49

Part III

Verbs

and

Tenses

Regular Verbs

Arabic has three tenses: past, present and imperative, (the form of command). The future is expressed by using the present tense. Arabic verbs are constructed from a root of three, occasionally four, letters (more on root words on pages 72 and 126). The different tenses are created by adding prefixes and suffixes to the root letters in addition to their vocalization.

Suffixes and prefixes added to the root also indicate the gender and number of the verb. For this reason, personal pronouns are usually omitted from a sentence as they are understood from the structure of the verb.

We have already discussed how to form simple non-verbal sentences. The other form, in Arabic, is the verbal sentence. A verbal sentence can consist of only a verb and a subject, or a verb, subject, and object. In most cases, a sentence will start with a verb followed by the subject and then the object.

Verbs are divided into regular and irregular forms. A regular verb is defined as one that does not include a *waaw*, *yaa'*, or *hamza* in its root and a verb where the second and third consonants are not identical.

In the following lessons, we will study how to form the past present and the imperative, how to express the future tense, and how to add pronoun suffixes to verbs. We will first introduce regular verbs, then we will study various examples of irregular verbs.

Before we start, here is a list of some common regular verbs. Verbs are given according to their root.

To search	baHatha	بَحَثَ
To leave	taraka	تَرَكَ
To pierce	thaqaba	ثَقَبَ
To attract	gadhaba	جَذَبَ
To calculate	Hasaba	حَسَبَ
To exit	kharaga	خَرَجَ
To study	darasa	دَرَسَ
To go	dhahaba	ذَهَبَ
To draw	rasama	رَسَمَ
To plant	zaraᶜa	زَرَعَ
To hear	samiᶜa	سَمِعَ
To witness	shahida	شَهِدَ
To ascend	Saᶜida	صَعِدَ
To laugh	DaHika	ضَحِكَ
To print	Tabaᶜa	طَبَعَ
To appear	Zahara	ظَهَرَ
To work	ᶜamila	عَمِلَ
To close	ghalaqa	غَلَقَ
To open	fataHa	فَتَحَ
To sit	qaᶜada	قَعَدَ
To write	kataba	كَتَبَ
To play	laᶜiba	لَعِبَ
To forbid	manaᶜa	مَنَعَ
To descend	nazala	نَزَلَ
To escape	haraba	هَرَبَ

53

PAST TENSE

The past tense, also referred to as the perfect tense, is used to express an action completed in the past. In Arabic, the past tense is formed by adding suffixes to the root word.

Let's look at the example كَتَبَ (kataba) or to write.

I wrote	anaa katabtu	أَنا كَتَبْتُ
You wrote (m,s)	anta katabta	أَنتَ كَتَبْتَ
You wrote (f,s)	anti katabti	أَنتِ كَتَبْتِ
He wrote	huwa kataba	هُوَ كَتَبَ
She wrote	hiya katabat	هِيَ كَتَبَتْ
We wrote	naHnu katabnaa	نحنُ كَتَبْنا
You wrote (m,p)	antum katabtum	أَنتُم كَتَبْتُم
You wrote (f,p)	antunna katabtunna	أَنتُنَّ كَتَبْتُنَّ
They wrote (m,p)	hum kataboo	هُم كَتَبُوا
They wrote (f,p)	hunaa katabna	هُنَّ كَتَبْنَ
You (m & f,d)	antumaa katabtumaa	أَنتُما كَتَبْتُما
They (m,d)	humaa katabaa	هُما كَتَبَا
They (f,d)	humaa katabataa	هُما كَتَبَتا

Ⓒ   Personal pronouns are usually omitted from a sentence since they can be understood from the structure of the verb. The following sentences convey the same meaning whether the personal pronoun is written or not.

EXAMPLES

I drank the coffee *anaa sharibtu al-qahwa*	أنا شربتُ القهوة
I drank coffee *sharibtu al-qahwa*	شربتُ القهوة
We watched the movie *naHnu shaahadnaa al-feelm*	نحن شاهدنا الفيلم
We watched the movie *shaahadnaa al-feelm*	شاهدنا الفيلم

Ⓒ   The verb comes first, followed by the subject. Sentences starting with a verb are referred to as a "verbal sentence." Some verbal sentences can have only a verb and a subject; others require a verb, subject, and an object.

EXAMPLES

Ahmed has travelled *saafara Ahmed*	سَافَرَ أحمد
The girl came *gaa't al-fataatu*	جاءت الفتاةُ
The thief escaped *haraba al-liSSu*	هَرَبَ اللصّ
Mona rode the car *rakibat Mona as-sayyaara*	رَكِبَت منى السيّارة
Ahmed opened the door *fataHa Ahmed al-baaba*	فتحَ أحمد البابَ
The boy played the ball *laʿiba al-waladu al-kura*	لَعِبَ الولدُ الكرةَ

Two Irregularities You Need to Study

First Irregularity: When a verb precedes the subject, the verb only agrees in gender with the subject, but not in number. In other words, the verb is written in the singular form, whether or not the subject is singular, dual, or plural.

Examples

رَقَصَت الفتاة في الحفل

The girl danced at the party
raqaSat al-fataah fee al-Hafl

رَقَصَت الفتيات في الحفل

The girls danced at the party
raqaSat al-fatayqat fee al-Hafl

ذهبت الفتيات إلى الحفل وجلسن

The girls went to the party and sat down
dhahabat al-fatayaat ilaa al-Hafl wa-galsna

رقصن في الحفل

They (f) danced at the party
raqSna fee al-Hafl

© In the first two examples, the verb (رقص) is given in the third person feminine singular, irrespective of the number of the noun.

© In the third example, the verb (ذهب) is conjugated in the singular form because it precedes the noun. However, the verb (جلس) is in the feminine plural form as it comes after the subject (the girls).

© In the fourth example, the subject is omitted from the sentence since it can be understood from the structure of the verb. In this case, the verb shows the gender and number of the subject it is referring to.

56

SECOND IRREGULARITY: The plural of inanimates is given in the third person feminine singular (she).

EXAMPLES

The plane landed *habaTat aT-Taa'ira*	هَبَطَتِ الطائرة
The planes landed *habaTat aT-Taa'iraat*	هَبَطَتِ الطائرات
The sparrow escaped from the cage *haraba al-ᶜuSfoor min al-qafaS*	هَرَبَ العصفور من القفص
The sparrows escaped from the cage *harabaT al-ᶜaSaafeer min al-qafaS*	هَرَبَتِ العصافير من القفص

In the above examples, note that the noun العصفور "the sparrow" is masculine. The verb given with its plural is in the third person feminine singular (*she*).

One point to remember if you want to dive into the intricacies of the Arabic grammar: The subject of the sentence is always in the nominative case. That is, it takes a *Damma* as a case ending if it is singular or a *waaw noon* ending if it is regular masculine plural. The object of the sentence is always in the accusative. That is, it takes a *fatHa* as a case ending if it is singular, or a *yaa' noon* if it is regular masculine plural.

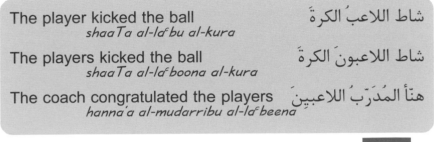

The player kicked the ball *shaaTa al-laᶜbu al-kura*	شاط اللاعبُ الكرةَ
The players kicked the ball *shaaTa al-laᶜboona al-kura*	شاط اللاعبونَ الكرةَ
The coach congratulated the players *hanna'a al-mudarribu al-laᶜbeena*	هنّأ المُدَرِّبُ اللاعبينَ

None of these Arabic sentences have a personal pronoun as
it is understood from the structure of the verb. These pronouns,
however, are missing from the English translation. Can you
find them and write them down?

I -- met yesterday
       taqablnaa bi-al-amsi

تقابلنا بالأمس

II -- married last year
        tazawgnaa al-ᶜaam al-maaDee

تزوجنا العام الماضي

III -- went to visit her friend
         dhahabat li-ziyaarat Sadeeqatihaa

ذَهَبَتْ لزيارة صديقتها

IV -- missed a golden opportunity
        faqadtum furSa dhahabiya

فقدتم فرصة ذهبية

V -- got a raise
       HaSala ᶜalaa ᶜilaawa

حصل على علاوة

VI -- laughed a lot
        DaHakna katheeran

ضحكنَ كثيراً

VII -- wrote their marriage contract
         katabaa al-kitaab

كَتبا الكتاب*

VIII -- listened to the new song
         samᶜtunna al-ughniya al-gadeeda

سَمَعتُنَّ الأغنية الجديدة

IX -- drank coffee
        sharibaa al-qahwa

شَربا القهوة

X -- drew a beautiful painting
       rasamat lawHa gameela

رَسَمَتْ لوحة جميلة

XI -- played in the garden
        laᶜibtu fee al-Hadeeqa

لَعِبتُ في الحديقة

This literally translates to "they wrote the book," but is a phrase
that commonly refers to signing a marriage contract.

PRESENT TENSE

Present tense, also known as the imperfect tense, refers to actions in the present and the present continuous. It can also refer to habitual actions and state of being. The present is formed by adding a set of prefixes and suffixes to the root word.

In this example, we will look at the verb كَتَبَ (kataba) to write.

I write	anaa aktubu	أَنا أَكْتُبُ
You write (m,s)	anta taktubu	أَنتَ تَكْتُبُ
You write (f,s)	anti taktubeena	أَنتِ تَكْتُبِينَ
He writes	huwa yaktubu	هُوَ يَكْتُبُ
She writes	hiya taktubu	هِي تَكْتُبُ
We write	naHnu naktubu	نَحنُ نَكْتُبُ
You write (m,p)	antum taktuboona	أَنتُم تَكْتُبُونَ
You write (f,p)	antunna taktubna	أَنتُنَّ تَكْتُبنَ
They write (m,p)	hum yaktuboona	هُم يَكْتُبُونَ
They write (f,p)	hunna yaktubna	هُنَّ يَكْتُبنَ
You write (f & m,d)	antumaa taktubaani	أَنتُما تَكْتُبانِ
They write (m,d)	humaa yaktubaani	هُمَا يَكْتُبانِ
They write (f,d)	humaa taktubaani	هُمَا تَكْتُبانِ

EXAMPLES

I run/am running
anaa arkuDu

أنا أركُضُ

He drinks
huwa yashrabu

هو يَشرَبُ

You (m) dream
antum taHlamoona

أنتم تحلمونَ

They (m) dance
hum yarquSoona

هم يَرقُصونَ

They (f) write
hunna yaktubna

هن يكتُبنَ

They (m) are listening to a new song
hum yasmaᶜoona ughniyatan gadeedatan

هم يَسمَعون أغنيةً جديدةً

They (f) work hard
hunna yaᶜmalna bi-nashaaT

هن يَعمَلنَ بنشاط

They (m) play the ball
yalᶜaboona al-kura

يَلعَبونَ الكرة

You listen to the music
anta tasmaᶜu al-mooseeqaa

أنت تَسمَعُ الموسيقى

They (f) study Arabic
yadrusna al-lugha al-ᶜarabiya

يَدرُسنَ اللغة العربية

The sun rises
tashruqu ash-shams

تَشرُقُ الشمس

They send their greetings
yabᶜathoona at-taHiya

يَبعَثونَ التحية

We work to eat
naᶜmalu li-na'kul

نَعمَلُ لنَأكُل

He always succeeds
yangaHu daa'iman

يَنجَحُ دائماً

He goes to work every morning
yadhhabu ilaa ᶜamalihi kul SabaaH

يَذهَبُ إلى عَمَلِهِ كل صباح

TALKING ABOUT THE FUTURE

Forming the future is easy. You simply add the Arabic word *sawfa* (سوف) to the verb in the present tense. Quite often, the word *sawfa* is shortened to a *seen* (سـ) and is attached as a prefix to the verb in the present tense.

EXAMPLES

I go to work *adhhabu ilaa al-ᶜamali*	أذهبُ إلى العملِ
I will go to work *sawfa adhhabu ilaa al-ᶜamali*	سوف أذهبُ إلى العملِ
I will go to work *sa-adhhabu ilaa al-ᶜamali*	سأذهبُ إلى العملِ

VOCABULARY

Tomorrow	*ghadan*	غداً
After tomorrow	*baᶜd ghad*	بعد غد
Next week	*al-usbooᶜ al-qaadim*	الأسبوع القادم
Next month	*ash-shahr al-qaadim*	الشهر القادم
Next year	*al-ᶜaam al-qaadim*	العام القادم
To marry	*zawwaga*	زوّج
Marriage	*zawaag*	زَواج
Joy/Wedding	*faraH*	فَرَح

سنتقابلُ غداً

We will meet tomorrow
sa-nataqaablu ghadan

سوف أزور أخي الأسبوع القادم

I will visit my brother next week
sawfa azooru akhee al-usbooᶜ al-qaadim

سوف أسَافرُ إلى الأردن الشهر القادم

I will travel to Jordan next month
sawfa usafiru ilaa al-urdunn ash-shahr al-qaadim

سوف أذهب مع صديقتي للتسوّق

I will go with my friend shopping
sawfa adhhabu maᶜa Sadeeqatee li-Itasawwuq

سوف نتزوج الأسبوع القادم وسنقيم فرحاً كبيراً

We will get married next week and we will hold a big wedding
sawfa natazawwagu al-usbooᶜ al-qaadim wa sa-nuqeemu faraHan kabeeran

☾ The future can also be expressed by using the present tense and a date in the future.

EXAMPLES

We will meet at 10 P.M.
naltaqee fee al-ᶜaashira masaa'n

نَلتقي فى العاشرة مساءً

Our meeting is tomorrow
mawᶜidnaa ghadan

موعدنا غداً

We will travel after tomorrow
nusaafiru baᶜd ghad

نُسافرُ بعد غد

We will meet tomorrow at the university
nataqaabalu ghadan fee al-gaamiᶜa

نتقابلُ غداً في الجامعةِ

Can you figure out the personal pronoun associated with these verbs? Write it down in the English translation.

I	-- know the truth	يَعلمُنَ الحقيقة
II	-- opens the door	يَفتحُ الباب
III	-- studies Arabic	يَدرسُ اللغة العربية
IV	-- studies French	تَدرسُ اللغة الفرنسية
V	-- ride the horses	نَركَبُ الخيل
VI	-- cook dinner	أطبُخُ الغذاء
VII	-- pours the juice	تَسكبُ العصير
VIII	-- will go to the movies	سوف يَذهبون إلى السينما
IX	-- always smiles	تَبتسمُ دائماً
X	-- will cook dinner	سوف أطبُخُ الغذاء
XI	-- will study French	سوف تَدرسُ اللغة الفرنسية
XII	-- will go to the theatre tomorrow	نَذهبُ غداً إلى المسرح
XIII	-- will travel to Beirut next week	أسافرُ الأسبوع القادم إلى بيروت

63

THE IMPERATIVE

The imperative is used to express a command. There are only six forms of the imperative, which are used to address the second person masculine singular, dual, and plural; and the second person feminine singular, dual, and plural. In spoken Arabic, the dual form and the feminine plural are hardly ever used.

The imperative is formed from the present tense. The prefix is omitted and an *alif* is added to the beginning of the verb.

☾ Here we will look at how to say the command "write" in Arabic, or verb (كَتَبَ) in the imperative:

You (m,s)	*uktub*	أُكتُب
You (f,s)	*uktubee*	أُكتُبي
You (m,d)	*uktubaa*	أُكتُبا
You (f,d)	*uktubaa*	أُكتُبا
You (m,p)	*uktuboo*	أُكتُبوا
You (f,p)	*uktubna*	أُكتُبنَ

EXAMPLES

Go (m,p)	*idhhaboo*	إذهَبوا
Listen (dual)	*ismaᶜaa*	اسمَعَا
Play (f,s)	*iʳabee*	العَبي
Get out (m,s)	*ukhrug*	أُخرُج
Ride (f,p)	*irkabna*	إركَبنَ

64

Place the verbs between brackets in their correct form.

ا   هو(يجلس) في المطعم أمس

I   He (sit) in the restaurant yesterday.

II   نحن سوف (يذهب) إلى المسرح غداً

II   We will (go) to the theatre tomorrow.

III   هي (يتدحدث) معه الآن

III   She (speak) with him now.

IV   هم (ينتظر) منذ الصباح

IV   They (m) (wait) since the morning.

V   هن (ينجح) دائماً

V   They (f) (succeed) always.

VI   هما (يضحك) كثيراً

VI   They (m,d) (laugh) a lot.

Change the following verbs to the present, past, and imperative.
The first example is done for you.

ا   (شرب) الضيف الشاي

يشرب الضيف الشاي

شرب الضيف الشاي

اشرب الشاي

II   هم (لعب) الكرة

III   (حدث) أختي

IV   (فتح) أحمد الباب

V   هن (ذهب) إلى السوق

VI   العروسان (كتب) الكتاب

65

IRREGULAR VERBS

An irregular verb is a verb that has one or more "weak" letters in its root. By a weak letter we mean either the *alif, waaw,* or *yaa'* (ي - و - ا). An irregular verb is also defined as a verb with identical second and third consonants, known as doubled verbs.

The tenses, gender, and number of irregular verbs share the same prefixes and suffixes as the regular ones. The main change occurs in the root itself. The pattern of conjugating an irregular verb depends on where the weak letter occurs in the verb's root. The pattern differs if the weak letter falls in the beginning, middle, or end of the verb. The pattern also differs if the weak letter is a *hamza, waaw,* or *yaa'.*

Depending on the pattern of the verb, you will notice that an irregular verb is sometimes conjugated regularly in the past and present tenses but will follow a different pattern in the imperative. At other times, the verb will be conjugated regularly in the past but not in the present. Note also that an irregular verb will be conjugated regularly with some pronouns but it will follow an irregular pattern for other pronouns.

For a beginner, it is not advisable to study tables of conjugated verbs in different patterns. It will be better to take note of these irregularities and the change in pattern. Learn each verb one at a time. In the following examples, we will look at some common weak verbs. Again, we suggest using the following pages only as a reference; do not attempt to memorize the verbs.

Examples of Irregular Verbs

Doubled verbs: These are verbs where the second and third letters are identical. The double letter is usually indicated by the *shadda* (see page 5).

كفَّ/شكَّ/ضلَّ/شدَّ/ملَّ/حبَّ

to stop/to doubt/to stray/to pull/to be bored/to love
kaffa/shakka/Dalla/shadda/malla/Habba

Hamzated verbs: These are verbs that have a *hamza* in their root, which can fall at the beginning, middle, or end of a word.

أخذ/أكل/ثأر/رأى/سأل/بدأ/قرأ

to take/to eat/to revenge/to see/to ask/to begin/to read
akhadha/akala/tha'ara/ra'aa/sa'ala/bada'a/qara'a

Weak Letter Verbs:

Verbs that start with a weak letter:

وَصَل/وَعَد/وَضَع/وَجَد/يَقِظَ

to connect/to promise/to put/to find/to wake
waSala/wa'ada/waDa'a/wagada/yaqiZa

Words that have a weak letter in the middle:

صَوَّرَ/خَيَّطَ/سَيطَرَ/لَوَّنَ/نَوَّرَ

to photograph/to sew/to dominate/to colour/to light
Sawwara/khayyaTa/sayTara/lawwana/nawwara

Verbs that end with a weak letter:

رَضِيَ/نَسِيَ/نَهى/رَمى

to accept/to forget/to forbid/to throw
raDiya/nasiya/nahaa/ramaa

EXAMPLES

© The verb أَخَذ (to take) starts with a *hamza*. It is conjugated regularly in the past and present. However, the *hamza* drops in the imperative. Verbs starting with a *hamza* are referred to as *hamzated* verbs.

They took the suitcases	*akhadhoo al-Haqaa'ib*	أَخَذُوا الحَقائِب
Take the suitcases	*khudh al-Haqaa'ib*	خُذ الحَقائِب

© The verb كَفّ (to stop) is a doubled verb. Instead of writing the last letter twice, this is indicated by the *shadda* (ّ). With certain pronouns, the double letters are written separately.

I stopped working	*kafaftu ᶜan al-ᶜamali*	كَفَفتُ عن العملِ
She stopped working	*kaffat ᶜan al-ᶜamali*	كَفَّت عن العملِ
Stop working (m,s)	*kuffa ᶜan al-ᶜamali*	كُفَّ عن العملِ

© In the verb باع (to sell), the weak letter changes into a *yaa'* in the present. In the past and in the imperative, the weak letter is dropped with certain pronouns. Verbs with a middle weak letter are known as hollow verbs.

I sold the car	*biᶜtu as-sayyaara*	بِعتُ السيّارة
I will sell the car	*sawfa abeeᶜu as-sayyaara*	سوف أبيعُ السيّارة
Sell the car (f,s)	*beeᶜee as-sayyaara*	بيعي السيّارة

© Another verb with a middle weak letter is the verb قال (to say/to tell). In the present, the *alif* changes into *waaw*. In the past and the imperative, the weak letter is dropped with certain pronouns.

He tells the truth	huwa yaqoulu al-Haqeeqa	هو يَقُولُ الحقيقة
He told the truth	huwa qaala al-Haqeeqa	هو قالَ الحقيقة
Tell (m,s) the truth	qul al-Haqeeqa	قُل الحقيقة

☾ Verbs starting with a weak letter— known as assimilated verbs—are conjugated regularly in the past tense. In the present and imperative, the weak letter is dropped. Here, we will look at the verb وعد (to promise).

I promised	anaa waʿadtu	أنا وَعَدتُ
I promise	anaa aʿidu	أنا أعِدُ
You (m,p) promised	antum waʿadtum	أنتم وَعَدتُم
You (m,p) promise	antum taʿidoona	أنتم تَعِدون
Promise (m,s)	ʿid	عِد

☾ Verbs with a final weak letter– known as defective verbs—follow several patterns. Most of the time, the verb is conjugated regularly in the past tense, with the sole exception of the third person masculine plural, they (m,p), where the weak letter is dropped. In the present tense, the weak letter is dropped for the third and second person masculine plurals— they (m,p) and you (m,p). Let's look at the verb رَضِيَ (to accept).

I accept	anaa arDaa	أنا أرضى
I accepted	anaa raDytu	أنا رَضيتُ
You (m,p) accept	antum tarDaoona	أنتم تَرضَونَ
You (m,p) accepted	antum raDaytum	أنتم رَضيتُم
They (m,p) accept	hum yarDoona	هم يرضون
They (m,p) accepted	hum raDoo	هم رضوا

69

☪ In some cases, the weak letter changes to the long vowel *waaw* or *yaa'*. Take note of these irregularities and learn to recognize them as you see new irregular verbs. Let's look at the verb دعا (to invite), which changes to دعو in the present tense.

I invite	anaa adʿoo	أنا أدعو
You (f,s) invite	anti tadʿeena	أنت تَدعين
He invites	huwa yadʿoo	هو يدعو
They (m) invite	huma yadʿuoona	هم يدعُون
I invited	anaa daʿawtu	أنا دَعَوتُ
You (f,s) invited	anti daʿawti	أنت دَعَوت
He invited	huwa daʿaa	هو دَعَا
They invited	hum daʿaoo	هم دَعَوا

☪ Some verbs have two weak letters in their root. In the following examples, we will look at the verb رأى to see.

I see	anaa araa	أنا أرَى
You (m,s) see	anta taraa	أنت ترَى
He sees	huwa yaraa	هو يرَى
We see	naHnu naraa	نحن نرَى
They see	hum yaraoona	هم يرَون
I saw	anaa ra'aytu	أنا رأيتُ
You (m,s) saw	anta ra'ayta	أنت رأيتَ
He saw	huwa ra'aa	هو رأى
We saw	naHnu ra'aynaa	نحن رأينَا
They saw	hum ra'aoo	هم رأوا

70

More irregular verbs (the root verb is given between brackets)

I cry	anaa abkee	أنا أُبكي (بَكَى)
We cry	naHnu nabkee	نحن نَبكي
They (m,p) cry	hum yabkuoona	هم يَبكُونَ
I cried	anaa bakytu	أنا بَكَيتُ
We cried	naHnu bakaynaa	نحن بَكَينا
They (m,p) cried	hum bakaoo	هم بكَوا
You (f,s) say	anti taqooleena	أنتِ تَقُولينَ (قَالَ)
She says	hiya taquoolu	هي تَقُولُ
You (f,s) said	anti qulti	أنتِ قُلتِ
She said	hiya qaalat	هي قَالَت
I eat	anaa aakulu	أنا آكُلُ (أَكَلَ)
We eat	naHnu na'akulu	نحن نَأكُلُ
I ate	anaa akaltu	أنا أكَلتُ
We ate	naHnu akalnaa	نحن أكلنا
Eat your food	kul Taᶜaamak	كُل طعامك
I was scared	anaa khuftu	أنا خُفتُ (خَافَ)
He was scared	huwa khaafa	هو خَافَ
I was suspicious	anaa shakaktu	أنا شَكَكتُ (شَكَّ)
He was suspicious	huwa shakka	هو شَكَّ

DERIVED FORMS OF THE VERB

We already discussed that Arabic verbs are composed of three, occasionally four, consonants. Now, from these three consonants, other verbs can be derived. These derived verbs are composed by adding one, two, or three extra letters to the root, following a specific pattern known as *al-mizan aS-Sarfy* (see page 135). These derived verbs usually share a common idea with their root. Different tenses are created by adding the same prefixes and suffixes as the root verb.

EXAMPLES

The root verb

to know	*ᶜalima*	عَلِمَ

Derived verbs

to inform - derived verb	*aᶜlama*	أَعْلَمَ
to inquire - derived verb	*istaᶜlama*	إِسْتَعْلَمَ

The root verb

to be awake	*yaqiZa*	يَقِظَ

Derived verbs

to wake (somebody) up	*ayqaZa*	أَيْقَظَ
to be vigilant	*tayaqqaZa*	تَيَقَّظَ
to wake up (from sleep)	*istayqaZa*	إِسْتَيْقَظَ

Root verb

to stop/to stand	*waqafa*	وَقَفَ

Derived verbs

to halt	*awqafa*	اوقَفَ
to bring to a stop	*istawqafa*	إِسْتَوْقَفَ

EXAMPLES

I witnessed the contract *shahidtu ᶜalaa al-ᶜaqd*	شَهِدتُ على العقد
I saw the new movie *shaahdtu al-feelm al-gadeed*	شَاهَدتُ الفيلم الجديد
I understood the lesson *fahimtu ad-dars*	فَهِمتُ الدرس
I inquired about this subject *istafhamtu ᶜan haadhaa al-mawDooᶜ*	إِستَفهَمتُ عن هذا الموضوع
The manager mentioned your name *al-mudeer dhaqara ismak*	المدير ذَكَرَ اسمك
The manager remembered your name *al-mudeer tadhakkara ismak*	المدير تَذَكَّرَ اسمك

VOCABULARY

English	Transliteration	Arabic
Traffic	*muroor*	مرور
Traffic light	*ishaarat al-muroor*	إشارة المرور
Police (s/p)	*shurTee/shurTa*	شرطي/شرطة
Fine	*mukhaalafa*	مخالفة
Event	*Hadath*	حدث
Accident	*Haadith*	حادث
To hit	*Sadama*	صدم
To collide, to crash	*iSTadama*	إصطدم
Collision	*taSaadum*	تصادم
Colleague/s	*zameel/zumalaa'*	زميل/ زملاء
Client, agent (s/p)	*ᶜameel/ᶜumalaa*	عميل/ عملاء
To quarrel	*tashaagara*	تَشَاجَرَ
To wear	*irtadaa*	إرتدى
To give	*aᶜTaa*	أعطى

73

نبيل: أين نذهب اليوم؟

Nabil: ayna nadhhabu al-yawm?

سامح: أريد أن أخرج وأنسى ماحدث لي أمس.

Sameh: ureedu an akhrug wa-ansaa maa Hadatha lee ams.

نبيل: ماذا حدث بالأمس؟

Nabil: maadhaa Hadatha bi-al-amsi?

سامح: قمتُ من النوم متأخّراً وكنت مستعجلاً وارتديت بالخطأ حذاءً أسود وآخر بني. وقدت السيّارة بسرعة وكدت أصدم رجلاً وزوجته وتشاجرا معي. ثمّ استوقفني رجلٌ شرطة وأعطاني مخالفة. ووصلتُ إلى عملي متأخّراً.

Sameh: qumtu min an-naoom muta'akhkhiran wa-kuntu mustaʿgilan wa-irtadeetu bi-al-khaTaa' Hidhaa'n aswad wa-aakhar bunee wa-qudtu as-sayyaara bi-surʿa wa-kudtu aSdimu ragulan wa-zawgatahu wa-tashaagaraa maʿee. thumma istawqafnee ragul shurTa wa-aʿTaanee mukhaalafa wa-waSaltu ilaa ʿamalee muta'akhkhiran.

نبيل: وماذا فعل زملائك؟

Nabil: wa-maadhaa faʿla zumalaa'ik?

سامح: تشاجروا معي. ونسيت موعد مع أهمّ عملاء الشركة ولم يرضوا عن عملي وكذلك مديرتي لم ترضَ عن عملي.

Sameh: tashaagaroo maʿee. wa-nasiytu mawʿid maʿa ahamm ʿumalaa' ash-sharika wa-lam yarDoo ʿan ʿamalee wa-kadhaalik mudeeratee lam tarDa ʿan ʿamalee.

نبيل: وبعد ذلك؟

Nabil : wa-baʿd dhaalika?

سامح: نسيت موعدي مع خطيبتي وتشاجرت معي.

Sameh: nasiytu mawʿidee maʿa khaTeebatee wa-tashaagarat maʿee.

نبيل: أعرف مكاناً مناسب لحالتك. هيا بنا.

Nabil: aʿrifu makaanan munaasib li-Haalatuk. hayaa binaa

In the boxes, you are given several derived verbs. Group together the verbs sharing the same root.

to be safe سلم I
_____
_____
_____

to go out/get out خرج II
_____
_____
_____

to share/
participate شرك III
_____
_____

to understand فهم IV
_____
_____
_____

to open فتح V
_____
_____
_____

to cut قطع VI
_____
_____

to calculate حسب VII
_____
_____

اشترك
to take part/to participate

استسلم
to surrender

تخرج
to graduate

تحسب
to be careful

شارك
to share

أفهم
to make someone understand

سالم
to keep peace

قاطع
to boycott

حاسب
to settle an account

استفتح
to commence

استخرج
to extract

استفهم
to inquire

تفتح
to open up

تفهّم
to try to understand

تفاهم
to understand each other

أخرج
to take out

فاتح
to speak first

سلّم
to deliver

استقطع
to deduct

أشرك
to make someone a partner

75

Tarek is living away from home. He heard that his father has earned a handsome sum of money from his work and decided to write him a letter. Put the verbs between brackets in their correct form and find out why Tarek has decided to write to his father.

عزيزي أبي

أنا (علم) أني لم (كتب) إليك منذ فترة طويلة. أنا (سمع) أنك (حصل) على ربح وفير من عملك. أنا (بعث) إليك بأرق تحية وأصدقائي أيضاً (بعث) إليك بتحيتهم. نحن (اريد) أن نأتي لنراك ولكن ليس لدينا سيّارة جديدة. وفي النهاية أنا (علم) أنك سوف (ذكر) عيد ميلادي.

مع خالص التحية
أبنك المخلص
طارق

zeezee abee

anaa (ᶜalima) anee lam (kataba) ilayka mundhu fatra Taweela. anaa (samiᶜa) anaka (HaSal) ᶜalaa ribH wafeer min ᶜamalak. anaa (baᶜtha) ilayka bi-araq taHiya wa-aSdiqaa'iee ayDan (baᶜatha) ilayka bi-taHiyatihum. naHnu (ureedu) an na'atee li-naraaka wa-lakin laysa ladaynaa sayyaara gadeeda. wa-fee an-nihaaya anaa (ᶜalima) anaka sawfa (zakara) ᶜeed meelaadee.
maᶜa khaliS at-taHiya
ibnaka al-mukhliS
Tarek

Nahed is trying to get her three children Ahmed, Reem, and Mona ready for bed. She is giving them a series of instructions. Can you find and underline the verbs in the imperative?

كفوا عن الخناق واشربوا اللبن ثمّ اغسلوا وجوهكم. منى وريم اذهبا إلى غرفتكما وأحمد اخلع ملابسك. والآن ناموا. لا انتظروا أعطوني قبلة ثمّ اذهبوا إلى النوم.

kufoo ᶜan al-khinaaq wa-ishraboo al-laban thumma aghsuloo wugoohakum. Mona wa-Reem idhhabaa ilaa ghurfatukumaa wa-Ahmed ikhlaᶜ malaabisak. wa-al'aan naamoo. la intaZuroo aᶜToonee qubla thumma idhhaboo ilaa an-nawm

VOCABULARY

The verb is given between brackets

Greetlng	*taHiya*	تحية
Profit/s	*ribH/arbaaH*	رِبح/أرباح
Abundant	*wafeer*	وفير
To receive	*HaSala*	حَصَلَ
The end	*an-nihaaya*	النهاية
Birthday	*ᶜeed meelaad*	عيد ميلاد
Fight (to fight)	*khinaaq (khanaqa)*	خِناق (خانقَ)
Sleep (to sleep)	*naama (nawm)*	نَامَ (نوم)
Clothes (to dress)	*malaabis (labisa)*	مَلابِس (لَبِسَ)
To wash	*ghasala*	غَسَلَ
To remove/take off	*khalaᶜa*	خَلَعَ
Kiss/es (to kiss)	*qubla/qubulaat (qabbala)*	قُبلة/ قُبُلات (قَبَّلَ)

77

VERBS AND PRONOUN ENDINGS

In English, the words me, you, him, her, it, us, and them are called object pronouns. In Arabic, object pronouns are added to a verb. Pronoun endings for verbs are the same as those discussed on page16, with the exception of the first person singular (I) which takes the possessive ending نِي.

Since personal pronouns do not need to be included with the verb, and the object of the verb is indicated by a suffix, you can make statements by using only one word.

EXAMPLES

She saw me *ra'atnee*	رأتني
He told her *akhbarahaa*	أخبرها
They heard us *sami'oonaa*	سمعونا
I understood him *fahimtuhu*	فهمته
I watched them *shaahidtuhum*	شاهدتهم
I love you *uHibbuka*	أحبّك
I drove him to the airport *waSSaltuhu ilaa al-maTaar*	وَصَّلتُه إلى المطار
He met her at the hotel *qabalahaa fee al-funduq*	قابلها في الفندق
I talked to them about the project *Haddaththuhum 'an al-mashroo'*	حدّثتهم عن المشروع
She hates him a lot *takrahuhu bi-shida*	تكرهه بشدة
Tell me about her *khabbrnee 'anhaa*	خبرني عنها
She taught us a lot *'allamatnaa al-katheer*	علّمتنا الكثير

All the verbs listed below have pronoun suffixes attached. Circle
the correct meaning of these words.

A. I heard him

B. I heard them

C. They heard us

سمعته ‏ا

A. I saw them

B. I saw her

C. She saw me

رأيتها ‏II

A. They heard us

B. We hear them

C. I hear them

نسمعهم ‏III

A. I understand them

B. They understand me

C. He understands them

يفهمهم ‏IV

A. They (d) saw us

B. I saw you (d)

C. He sees them

شاهدتكما ‏V

A. This news made us happy

B. This news will make him happy

C. This news made me happy

هذا الخبر فرحني ‏VI

PART IV

INTERROGATIVE, PREPOSITIONS, AND NEGATION

INTERROGATIVE

Interrogative words ask questions about someone, something, time, or state. This is a list of interrogative terms.

When	*mataa*	مَتى
What	*maa*	ما
What *(used before verbs)*	*maadhaa*	مَاذا
Why	*li-maadhaa*	لِمَاذا
Where	*ayna*	أَيْنَ
How much/How many	*kam*	كَمْ
Who	*man*	مَنْ
Which (m)	*ayy*	أيّ
Which (f)	*ayya*	أَيَّة
How	*kayfa*	كَيْفَ
Interrogative particle*	*hal*	هَل

* Introduces a question that requires a yes or no answer. Equivalent to: is, are, or did.

ANSWER WORDS

Yes	*naʿam*	نَعَم
No	*laa*	لاَ
Yes, indeed*	*balaa*	بَلَى

* Not commonly used. Generally used to respond to a negative question.

VOCABULARY

Watch/Hour	sadʿa	ساعة
Time	waqt	وَقت
Language	lugha	لُغة
To cry	bakaa	بَكى
To laugh	DaHaka	ضَحَكَ
To leave	ghaadara	غادَرَ
To come/To arrive	ataa	أتى
Arrival	wuSool	وصول
Exit	khuroog	خُروج
Show	ʿarD	عَرض
Meeting	liqaaʾ	لقاء
Monkey/Monkeys	qird/qurood	قِرد/قُرود
Statue	timthaal	تمثال
Thief/Thieves	liSS/liSooS	لصّ/الصوص
Midnight	muntaSif al-layl	منتصف الليل
Window/Windows	naafidha/nawaafidh	نافذة/نوافذ
Partner/Partners	shareek/shurakaaʾ	شريك/شركاء
Not yet	laysa baʿd	ليس بعد
Priceless	laa yuqaddir bi-thaman	لايقدّر بثمن
Museum/Museums	matHaf/mataaHif	متحف/متاحف

83

Do you have a room?
hal ladaykum ghurfa?
هل لديكم غرفة؟

Where are you?
ayna ant?
أين أنت؟

What are you saying?
maadhaa taqoolu?
ماذا تقولُ؟

When will the show begin?
mataa yabda'a al-ᶜarD?
متى يبدأ العرض؟

What time does the show begin?
fee ayyata saaᶜa yabda'a al-ᶜarD?
في أيَّة ساعة يبدأ العرض؟

Where can I rent a car?
ayna yumkin an asta'agiru sayyaara?
أين يمكن أن أستأجر سيّارة؟

How are you?
kayfa Haaluka?
كَيف حالكَ؟

Do you (f,s) speak English?
hal tataHaddatheena al-ingliziya?
هل تتَحدَّثينَ الإنجليزية ؟

Can you help me?
hal yumkin an tusaaᶜdunee?
هل يمكن أن تساعدني؟

Why are you late?
li-maadhaa ta'akhart?
لماذا تأخرت؟

Which food do you like?
ayy Taᶜaamin tuHib?
أيّ طعامٍ تحب؟

How many languages do you speak?
kam lughatan tataHaddath?
كم لغةً تتَحدّث؟

What is your favourite book?
maa huwa kitaabuka al-mufaDal?
ماهو كتابك المفضل؟

Why are you crying?
li-maadhaa tabkee?
لماذا تبكي؟

Why are you avoiding me?
li-maadhaa tataharrabu minee?
لماذا تتَهرّب مني؟

Who is speaking?
man yataHddath?
من يَتَحدّث؟

Fill in the blank with the proper interrogative particle. Use the English translation to help you.

Where are you?	I -- أنت؟
Who is she?	II -- هي؟
How are you?	III -- حالك؟
Where is the car?	IV -- السيارة؟
Do you have a room?	V -- لديكم غرفة؟
Who is speaking (f)?	VI - تتحدث؟
How much do you earn in one day?	VII -- تكسب في اليوم؟
What is your name?	VIII --اسمك؟
Where is the restaurant?	IX -- المطعم؟
What time do you wake up?	X في--ساعة تستيقظ؟
How much is this ring?	XI -- ثمن هذا الخاتم؟
Can you repeat the question?	XII -- يمكن أن تعيد السؤال؟
When did you come and where are you staying?	XIII أتيت و-- تمكث؟

THE GRAND THEFT

Thieves have managed to break into the museum and steal a priceless statue. The police detective is holding a press conference and reluctantly answers the journalists' questions.

صحفي١: ماذا حدث؟
SaHafee1: maadhaa Hadatha?

مفتّش المباحث: اقتحم لصّ المتحف
Mufattish al-mabaaHith: iqtaHam liSS al-matHaf

صحفي٢: متى حدثت السرقة؟
SaHafee2: mataa Hadathat as-sariqa?

مفتّش المباحث: مساء أمس
Mufattish al-mabaaHith: masaa´ ams

صحفي٣: في أية ساعة؟
SaHafee3: fee ayyata saaᶜa?

مفتّش المباحث: بعد منتصف الليل
Mufattish al-mabaaHith: baᶜd muntaSif al-layl

صحفي ٤: هل قبضتم على اللصّ؟
SaHafee4: hal qabaDtum ᶜalaa al-liSS?

مفتّش المباحث: نعم
Mufattish al-mabaaHith: naᶜam.

صحفي ٤: ما هي مواصفاته؟
SaHafee4: maa hiya muwaaSafaatuhu?

مفتّش المباحث: شاب قصير القامة وبدين جدّاً
Mufatiish al-mabaaHith: shaab qaseer al-qaama wa-badeen giddan.

صحفي ١: هل سرق شئ من المتحف؟
SaHafee1: hal saraqa shay´ min al-matHaf?

مفتّش المباحث: نعم تمثال أثري ثمين
Mufattish al-mabaaHith: naᶜam timthaal atharee thameen

صحفي٣: كم ثمن هذا التمثال؟

SaHafee3: kam thaman haadhaa at-timthaal?

مفتّش المباحث: لايقدّر بمال

Mufattish al-mabaaHith: laa yuqaddir bi-maal

صحفي٤: هل وجدتم التمثال؟

SaHafee4: hal wagadtum at-timthaal?

مفتّش المباحث: لا ليس بعد

Mufattish al-mabaaHith: laa laysa ba‘d

صحفي ١: كيف اقتحم اللصّ المتحف؟

SaHafee1: kayfa iqtaHam al-liSS al-matHaf?

مفتّش المباحث: قفز من نافذة صغيرة

Mufattish al-mabaaHith: qafaza min naafidha Sagheera

صحفي٣: وكيف قفز شاب بدين جدّاً من نافذة صغيرة؟

SaHafee3: wa-kayfa qafaza shaab badeen giddan min naafidha Sagheera?

مفتّش المباحث: كان معه شريك

Mufattish al-mabaaHith: kaana ma‘hu shareek

صحفي٤: ومن هذا الشّريك؟

SaHafee4: wa-man haadhaa ash-shareek?

مفتّش المباحث: آ آ آ آ قرد

Mufattish al-mabaaHith: ah ah ah ah qird

صحفي ٢: قرد! وهل قبضتم على القرد؟

SaHafee2: qird! wa-hal qabaDtum ‘alaa al-qird?

مفتّش المباحث: لا ليس بعد

Mufattish al-maabaHith: laa laysa ba‘d

Prepositions

A preposition is a word used to express a noun's or pronoun's relation to other words in a sentence. A preposition generally defines location, direction, or duration of its noun. In Arabic, prepositions are known as *huruf al-garr* (genitive letters) since a word following a preposition is always in the genitive. Arabic prepositions are either separate or attached. A separate preposition is a word that comes before a noun. An attached preposition is a letter connected to the noun.

Separate Prepositions

In, at	*fee*	فِي
From	*min*	مِنْ
On	*ᶜalaa*	عَلَى
To	*ilaa*	إِلَى
About, away from	*ᶜan*	عَنْ
With	*maᶜa*	مَعَ

Attached Prepositions

For, to	*li*	لِ
By, with, at, in	*bi*	بِ
Like, as	*ka*	كَ
By (of oath)*	*wa*	وَ

Very rarely used, do not confuse it with the conjunction letter waaw (و) which translates to "and".

I live in Australia *a'eeshu fee usturaaliyaa*	أعيش في أستراليا
I am from Canada *anaa min canadaa*	أنا من كندا
I travelled from Beirut to Cairo *saafartu min bayroot ilaa al-qaahira*	سافرتُ من بيروت إلى القاهرة
He travelled by train *saafara bi-al-qiTaari*	سافرَ بالقطارِ
The book is on the shelf *al-kitaab 'alaa ar-raffi*	الكتاب على الرفّ
We met at the university *taqaabalnaa fee al-gaami'ati*	تَقَابَلنَا في الجامعةِ
Successful like his father *naagiH ka-abeehi*	ناجح كأبيهِ
By God, I won't let you go *wa-allahi lan atrukak*	واللهِ لن أتركك

☾ Most of the following words are referred to in English as prepositions but are known in Arabic as adverbs of place.

In front of	amaama	أمَام
Behind	khalfa	خَلفَ
Above	fawqa	فَوقَ
Under	taHta	تَحتَ
After	ba'da	بَعدَ
Towards	naHwa	نَحوَ
Between	bayna	بَين
Right	yameen	يمين
Left	yasaar	يَسار
At, near	'inda	عند

EXAMPLES

I stand in front of the door *anaa aqifu amaama al-baab*	أنا أقف أمام الباب
The bag is under the bed *al-Haqeeba taHta as-sareer*	الحقيبة تحت السرير
He kicked the ball outside the goal *shaaTa al-kura khaariga al-marmaa*	شاط الكرة خارج المرمى
He kicked the ball toward the goal *shaaTa al-kura naHwa al-marmaa*	شاط الكرة نحو المرمى
I sat between my in-laws *galastu bayna Hamaatee wa-Hamaaee*	جلست بين حماتي وحماي

VOCABULARY

To search	*baHatha*	بَحَثَ
To find	*wagada*	وَجَدَ
To forget	*nasiya*	نَسِيَ
Glasses	*naZZaara*	نظّارة
Closet/Closets	*doolaab/dawaaleeb*	دولاب/دواليب
Box/Boxes	*Sundooq/Sanaadeeq*	صندوق/اصناديق
Key/Keys	*miftaaH/mafaateeH*	مفتاح/مفاتيح
Shelf/Shelves	*raff/rufoof*	رفّ/رفوف
To drive	*qaada*	قَادَ
To help	*saaʿada*	سَاعَدَ
To carry	*Hamala*	حَمَلَ
Speed	*surʿa*	سرعة
To comment	*ʿallaqa*	عَلّقَ
To study (to remember)	*dhaakara*	ذاكَرَ (ذكر)

90

Sami misplaced his glasses and asked his mother to help him find them. Sami's mother is clearly irritated, but gives him the following instructions. Can you underline the prepositions and figure out where Sami's glasses are?

اذهب إلى غرفتك وابحث عن مفتاح الدولاب وبالدولاب يوجد رفّ وعلى الرفّ يوجد صندوق وفي الصندوق توجد النظارة. سامي أنت تنسى دائماً كأبيك!

Fill in the blanks with the proper preposition. The English translation is provided to help you.

I stay with my Friends	أقيم -- أصدقائي ١
She is from America	هي -- أمريكا ١١
I won't comment on this question	لن أعلق -- هذا السؤال ١١١
Study to succeed	ذاكر -تنجح ١٧
I have to speak with Sarah	يجب أن أتحدث - -سارة ٧
Talk to me about Ahmed	حدثني -- أحمد ٧١
She drives with too much speed	هي تقود -سرعة جنونية ٧١١
I do not like to go to work	لا أحب الذهاب -- العمل ٧١١١

Prepositions and Pronoun Suffixes

Prepositions can take pronoun suffixes. The suffixes are the same as those covered on page 16. When a suffix is attached to a preposition, it indicates its object.

Examples

On the bed	ʿalaa as-sareer	على السَرير

If you have already referred to the bed you can say:

On it	ʿalayhi	عليه
In th box	fee aS-Sundooq	في الصندوق
In it	feehi	فيهِ
I miss Mona	ashtaaqu ilaa Mona	أشتاق إلى منى
I miss her	ashtaaqu ilayhaa	أشتاق إليها
We ask about Ahmed	nasa'alu ʿan Ahmed	نسأل عن أحمد
We ask about him	nasa'alu ʿanhu	نسأل عنه
I went out with Hoda	kharagtu maʿa Hoda	خَرجتُ مع هدى
I went out with her	kharagtu maʿahaa	خَرجتُ معها
The car is for Ahmed	as-sayyaara li-Ahmed	السيّارة لأحمد
The car is for him	as-sayyaara lahu	السيّارة له

VOCABULARY

Feeling sick

Illness/Disease	maraD	مَرَض
Patient (m/f)	mareeD/mareeDa	مَريض/مَريضة
Pain	alam	ألَم
Chest pain	alam fee aS-Sadr	ألَم في الصَدر
Back pain	alam fee aZ-Zahr	ألَم في الظَهر
Stomach pain	alam fee al-maᶜida	ألَم في المَعِدة
Headache	Sudaaᶜ	صُداع
Operation	ᶜamaliya	عَمَلية
Fracture	kasr	كَسر
Fever	Hummaa	حُمّى
Flu	infulwanzaa/zukaam	إنفلونزا/زكام
Cough	suᶠaal	سُعال
Medical examination	kashf Tibbee	كشف طبّي
Medicine	dawaa'	دَواء
Pharmacy	Saydaliya	صَيدَلية
Prescription	rooshita	روشتة
To cure	shafaa	شَفى
Cure	shifaa'	شِفاء
Hospital	mustashfaa	مُستَشفى
Emergency room	ghurfat aT-Tawaari'	غُرفة الطَوارئ
Ambulance	isᶜaaf	إسعاف
I have	ᶜindee	عَندي

DIALOGUE

Youssef is not feeling well, so he goes to the doctor for a medical examination. Read this dialogue and take note of the pronoun suffixes attached to prepositions.

دكتور: ماذا بك؟

Doctoor: maadhaa bika?

يوسّف: عندي ألم في جسمي وصداع في رأسي

Youssef: ᶜindee alam fee gismee wa-Sudaᶜ fee ra'see

دكتور: ولكَ على هذا الحال فترة طويلة؟

Doctoor: wa-laka ᶜalaa haadhaa al-Haal fatra Taweela?

يوسّف: لي على هذا الحال أسبوع

Youssef: lee ᶜalaa haadhaa al-Haal usbooᶜ

دكتور: تفضّل على السرير. اِسترح عليه

Doctoor: tafaDDal ᶜalaa as-sareer. istariH ᶜalayhi

(بعد الكشف)

(baᶜd al-kashf)

دكتور: عندكَ حمّى عليكَ بالراحة التّامة

Doctoor: ᶜindaka Hummaa ᶜaleeka bi-ar-raaHa at-taama

يوسّف: هل أحتاج إلى دواء؟

Yoususef: hal aHtaagu ilaa dawaa'?

دكتور: نعم. تفضّل هذا الدواء فيه الشفاء بإذن الله

Doctoor: naᶜam. tafaDDal haadhaa ad-dawaa' feehi ash-shifaa' bi-idhn allah

يوسّف: شكراً يادكتور سعدتُ بلقاءك.

Youssef: shukran ya-doctoor saᶜidtu bi-liqaa'k

94

NEGATION

In Arabic, the particle (word) used to make a sentence negative differs depending on whether the sentence is in the past, present, or future.

No/not	*laa*	لا
used to negate the present		
Not	*maa*	ما
used to negate the past/present		
Not	*lam*	لم
used with the past tense		
Not	*lan*	لن
used with the future tense		
Not to be/it is not	*laysa*	ليس
used to negate a nominal sentences		

SAYING NO IN THE PRESENT

The simplest way of forming a negative sentence is to add the particle لا (*laa*) before the verb in the present tense.

EXAMPLES

I don't understand the lesson
laa afhamu ad-dars
لاأفهمُ الدرس

They don't speak Arabic
laa yataHadathoona al-ᶜarabiya
لايتحدّثونَ العربية

He doesn't talk to me
laa yatakallamu maᶜee
لايَتكلّمُ معي

She doesn't want to go out
laa tureedu an takhrug
لاتريدُ أن تخرج

Saying No in the Past

There are two ways to negate the past. You can use *maa* (ما) and the verb in the past tense, or you can use *lam* (لم) and the verb in the present tense.

Examples

I did not like the movie *maa aHbabtu al-feelma*	ما أحببت الفيلم
I did not like the movie *lam uHibb al-feelma*	لم أحبّ الفيلم

Ⓒ Notice that, in the first example, the verb (حبّ) is in the past tense. In the second example, the verb is given in the present.

Saying No in the Future

To negate the future, you use *lan* (لن) with the verb in the present tense.

Examples

I will not speak to Ahmed *lan ataHaddatha maᶜa Ahmed*	لن أتحدّثَ مع أحمد
I do not speak to Ahmed *laa ataHaddathu maᶜa Ahmed*	لا أتحدّثُ مع أحمد
I did not speak to Ahmed *maa taHaddathtu maᶜa Ahmed*	ماتحدّثتُ مع أحمد
lam ataHaddath maᶜa Ahmed	لم أتحدّث مع أحمد

Ⓒ The first example is negating the future. The second is negating the present tense. The last two examples show two possible ways of negating the past tense.

NEGATING A NOMINAL SENTENCE

To negate a nominal sentence—a sentence with no verb—
you use the particle *laysa* (ليس).

EXAMPLES

The house is clean *ul-baytu naZeefun*	البيتُ نظيفٌ
The house is not clean *laysa al-baytu naZeefan**	ليس البيتُ نظيفاً
The film is funny *al-feelmu muDHikun*	الفيلم مضحك
The film is not funny *laysa al-feelmu muDHikan**	ليس الفيلم مضحكاً

** A note to the advanced learner: The predicate of the
sentence starting with laysa is always in the accusative case.*

OTHER WORDS THAT EMPHASIZE THE NEGATIVE

Never	*abadan*	أبداً
Nobody	*laa aHad*	لاأحد
Not yet	*laysa baᶜd*	ليس بعد
Nothing	*laa shay'*	لاشئ
There is nothing	*laa yoogad*	لايوجد
Impossible	*mustaHeel*	مستحيل
Unbelievable	*laa maᶜqool*	لامعقول
Without	*bidoon*	بِدون

97

On a Positive Note

Always	daa'iman	دائماً
Sometimes	aHyaanan	احياناً
Often	ᶜaadatan	عادةً
Possible	mumkin	ممكن
Really	fiᶜlan	فعلاً

Vocabulary

Dress/es	fustaan/fasaateen	فستان/فساتين
Shoe/s	Hidhaa'/aHdhiya	حذاء/أحذية
Shirt/s	qameeS/qumSaan	قميص/قمصان
Belt/s	Hizaam/aHzima	حزام/أحزمة
Suit/s	badla/bidal	بدلة/إبدَل
Sock/s	gawrab/gawaarib	جورب/جوارِب
Underwear	malaabis daakhiliya	ملابس داخلية
Skirt	jeeb (gonnella)	جيب (جونلة)
Trousers (s/p)	banTaloon/banTaloonaat	بنطلون/بنطلونات
Tie	rabTat ᶜunq (kravata)	ربطة عنق (كرافتة)
Suitable	munaasib	مُناسب
Shopping	tasawwuq	تَسَوّق
Market	sooq/aswaaq	سوق/أسواق
Wide	waasiᶜ	واسع
Tight	Dayyiq	ضَيّق
Now	al'aan	الآن
Solution	Hall	حلّ

98

EXERCISE 1

Laila is going out tonight. She is looking through her closet but there is nothing she likes. Follow what she is saying and mark the negative.

لا أعرف ماذا أرتدي اليوم لن أرتدي الفستان الأزرق انه ضيق والفستان الأحمر لم أعد أحبّه اما الفستان الأخضر لم يعد يناسبني. والفستان الأصفر واسع جدّاً. ولن أرتدي الأسود انا ماأحببت الأسود ابداً. لايوجد شئ آخر أرتديه. حسناً لايوجد حلّ غير ان أذهب إلى التسوّق ولكن ماذا أرتدي الآن !

EXERCISE 2

Negate the following sentences.

I will go to the cinema	سوف أذهب إلى السينما	١
I heard the latest news	سمعت آخر الأخبار	١١
I understand the lesson	أفهم الدرس	١١١
I will travel to Morocco tomorrow	أسافر غداً إلى المغرب	١٧
I speak Arabic	أتحدث العربية	٧
I went out with Mona yesterday evening	خرجت مع منى مساء أمس	٧١

99

PART V

NUMBERS, TIME, DAYS AND MONTHS

NUMBERS

Arabic numbers are a tricky subject to study for the following reasons: Like nouns and adjectives, numbers have masculine and feminine forms; rules governing number and gender agreement are marred with irregularities; grammatical rules are often ignored in spoken Arabic; and numbers are pronounced differently from their written form. In the following pages we will try, as much as possible, to simplify the rules.

It is important to note that whereas Arabic is written from right to left, numbers are written from left to right.

Year 2008   عام ٢٠٠٨

CARDINAL NUMBERS (0–10)

The masculine form is given first, followed by the feminine.

0	Sifr	صفر	٠
1	waaHid/waaHida	واحد/واحدة	١
2	ithnaan/ithnataan	اِثنان/اِثنتان	٢
3	thalaath/thalaatha	ثلاث/ثلاثة	٣
4	arbaᶜ/arbaᶜa	أربع/أربعة	٤
5	khams/khamsa	خمس/خمسة	٥
6	sitt/sitta	ستّ/ستّة	٦
7	sabᶜ/sabᶜa	سبع/سبعة	٧
8	thamaanin/thamaaniya	ثمان/ثمانية	٨
9	tisᶜ/tisᶜa	تسع/تسعة	٩
10	ᶜashar/ᶜashara	عشر/عشرة	١٠

Notes on Numbers 1–10

Numbers 1 and 2 agree in gender with their noun. Since Arabic has a dual form, the dual ending is used to refer to the number 2. In most cases, the number 1 is also omitted from a sentence, as it is understood from the structure of the noun.

One dollar=dollar	*doolaar waaHid=doolaar*	دولار واحد = دولار
Two dollars	*doolaaraan*	دولاران
One lira	*leera*	ليرة
Two liras	*leerataan*	ليرتان

☾ An irregularity in Arabic occurs with numbers 3–10: They do not agree in gender with their nouns. Also, the noun following numbers 3–10 is written in the plural form and in the genitive.

Examples

Three men
thalaathatu rigaalin
ثلاثةُ رجالٍ

Three girls
thalaathu banaatin
ثلاثُ بناتٍ

He speaks four languages
yataHaddathu arbaᶜ lughaatin
يتحدّثَ أربعَ لغاتٍ

I see five boys
araa khamsata awlaadin
أرى خمسةَ أولادٍ

Three nights and four days
thalaathu layaalin wa-arbaᶜatu ayyaamin
ثلاثُ ليالٍ وأربعةُ أيّام

Cardinal Numbers (11 – 19)

Numbers 11 to 19 are formed by adding عشر (ᶜashar) for the masculine, or عشرة (ᶜashara) for the feminine.

11	aHada ᶜashara/ iHdaa ᶜashrata	١١ أَحَدَ عَشَرَ/ إحدَى عَشْرَةَ
12	ithnaa ᶜashara/ ithnataa ᶜashrata	١٢ اثنَا عَشَرَ/اثنَتَا عَشرَةَ
13	thalaathata ᶜashara/ thalaatha ᶜashrata	١٣ ثَلاثَةَ عَشَرَ/ ثَلاثَ عَشرَةَ
14	arbaᶜata ᶜashara/ arbaᶜa ᶜashrata	١٤ أربَعَةَ عَشَرَ/أربَعَ عَشرَةَ
15	khamsata ᶜashara/ khamsa ᶜashrata	١٥ خَمسَةَ عَشَرَ/خَمسَ عَشرَةَ
16	sittata ᶜashara/ sitta ᶜashrata	١٦ سِتَّةَ عَشَرَ/سِتَّ عَشرَةَ
17	sabᶜata ᶜashara/ sabᶜa ᶜashrata	١٧ سَبعَةَ عَشَرَ/سَبعَ عَشرَةَ
18	thamaaniyata ᶜashara/ thamaaniya ᶜashrata	١٨ ثَمَانِيَةَ عَشَرَ/ثَمَانِي عَشرَةَ
19	tisᶜata ᶜashara/ tisᶜa ᶜashrata	١٩ تِسعَةَ عَشَرَ/تِسعَ عَشرَةَ

Notes and Examples

☾ The tens part of the number agrees with the counted noun in gender, but the unit part does not. Nouns are written in their singular forms and in the accusative.

Three days	thalaathatu ayyaamin	ثلاثةُ أيَّامٍ
Thirteen days	thalaathata ᶜashara yawman	ثلاثةَ عشرَ يوماً
Thirteen nights	thalaatha ᶜasharta laylatan	ثلاثَ عشرةَ ليلةً

☾ In the previous examples, note that the noun يوم (day) is written in its plural form with numbers 3–10 and in its singular form with teen numbers.

104

Multiples of Ten up to 100

20	ʿishroon	عِشرُونَ	٢٠
30	thalaathoon	ثَلاثونَ	٣٠
40	arbaʿoon	أربعونَ	٤٠
50	khamsoon	خَمسونَ	٥٠
60	sittoon	سِتّونَ	٦٠
70	sabʿoon	سَبعونَ	٧٠
80	thamaanoon	ثَمانونَ	٨٠
90	tisʿoon	تِسعونَ	٩٠
100	miʾa	مئة (مائة)	١٠٠

☾ Multiples of ten from 20 to 90 have only one form for both masculine and feminine.

| Twenty nights | ʿishroon laylatan | عشرون ليلةً |
| Thirty days | thalaathoon yawman | ثلاثون يوماً |

Large Numerals

Thousand	alf	ألف ١٠٠٠
Million	milyoon	مليون
Billion	milyaar (bilyoon)	مليار (بليون)

☾ Large numerals also have one form for both masculine and feminine.

| One thousand liras | alf leera | ألف ليرة |
| One million dinar | milyoon deenaar | مليون دينار |

105

Adding units to the tens

Compound numbers, such as 21, 32, are formed by adding the tens with smaller numbers, using the *waaw* (و) to connect.

21	*waaHid wa-ᶜishroon*	واحد وعشرون	٢١
32	*ithnaan wa-thalaathoon*	اثنان وثلاثون	٣٢
43	*thalaatha wa-arbaᶜoon*	ثلاثة وأربعون	٤٣
54	*arbaᶜa wa-khamsoon*	أربعة وخمسون	٥٤
65	*khamsa wa-sittoon*	خمسة وستّون	٦٥
76	*sitta wa-sabᶜoon*	ستّة وسبعون	٧٦
87	*sabᶜa wa-thamaanoon*	سبعة وثمانون	٨٧
98	*thamaaniya wa-tisᶜoon*	ثمانية وتسعون	٩٨
101	*miᵃa wa-waaHid*	مئة وواحد	١٠١
212	*miᵃataan wa-ithnaa ᶜashar*	مئتان واثنا عشر	٢١٢

ⓒ These numbers are used with a masculine noun. If you are referring to a feminine noun, drop the *taa' marbooTa* from the unit numbers. In spoken Arabic, the form given above is the one used for both masculine and feminine nouns.

Examples

Twenty five books
khamsa wa-ᶜishroon kitaaban
خمسة وعشرون كتاباً

Twenty four hours
arbaᶜ wa-ᶜishroon saaᶜa
أربع وعشرون ساعة

In twenty four hours
fee arbaᶜ wa-ᶜishreen saaᶜa
في أربع وعشرين ساعة*

* Compound numbers take case endings—the waaw noon in the nominative and yaa' noon in the accusative and genitive. In spoken Arabic, the yaa' noon (ين) ending is generally used.

106

Fractions

Tenth	ʿushr	عُشر
Eighth	thumn	ثُمن
Sixth	suds	سُدس
Fifth	khums	خُمس
Quarter	rubʿ	رُبع
Third	thulth	ثُلث
Half	niSf	نِصف
Two-thirds	thultheen	ثُلثين
Three-quarters	thalaathatu arbaaʿ	ثلاثة أرباع
One Hundred Percent	miʾa bi-al-miʾa	مئة بالمئة

Examples

One-tenth of the salary	ʿushr ar-raatib	عُشر الراتب
Quarter of an Hour	rubʿ saaʿa	رُبع ساعة
Half a kilo	niSf keelo	نِصف كيلو
Fifth of a litre	khums litr	خُمس لتر
One-eighth of a pound	thumn raTl	ثُمن رطل
Half the time	niSf al-waqt	نِصف الوقت
100%	miʾa bi-al-miʾa	١٠٠٪
1/4 of a million	rubʿ milyoon	١/٤ مليون

107

NUMBERS IN SPOKEN ARABIC

Most Arabic speakers do not strictly adhere to grammatical rules. Spoken (and informally written rules) differ from written ones.

☪ It is not important to spell out the numbers, especially for numbers above ten. Most native speakers write the figure format.

502 pounds	*khumsumeea wa-ithneen ginayh*	٥٠٢ جنيه
24 hours	*arbaᶜa wa-ᶜishreen sadᶜa*	٢٤ ساعة

☪ Arabic speakers simplify the rules behind the number/gender agreement. They use the feminine form when counting (number 1 and 2 are counted using the masculine form). The feminine form is generally used to express amounts and quantities. Nouns are also normally given in their singular form.

Five dollars	*khamsa doolaar*	خمسة دولار
Six liras	*sitta leera*	ستّة ليرة
Ten dinars	*ᶜashra deenaar*	عشرة دينار

☪ When referring to teen numbers (11–19), the unit and the ten are usually assimilated together and pronounced as one word.

Fourteen	أربعة عشر ← أربعتاشر
	arbaᶜatu ᶜashar → arbᶜtaashar

☪ Compound numbers and multiples of ten (20, 30, etc.) are pronounced using *the yaa' noon* (ين) case ending.

Twenty five books
خمسة وعشرون كتاباً ← خمسة وعشرين كتاب
khamsa wa-ᶜishroon kitaaban → khamsa wa-ᶜishreen kitaab

ORDINAL NUMBERS

Ordinal numbers are used to show an order or position (eg: first, second, etc). In Arabic, ordinal numbers are either masculine or feminine, they agree in gender with their noun.

First
al-awwal/al-uwlaa

الأوّل/الأولى

Second
ath-thaanee/ath-thaaniya

الثّاني/الثّانِيَة

Third
ath-thaalith/ath-thaalitha

الثّالِث/الثّالِثَة

Fourth
ar-raabiᶜ/ar-raabiᶜa

الرّابِع/الرّابِعَة

Fifth
al-khaahmis/al-khaamisa

الخَامِس/الخَامِسَة

Sixth
as-saadis/as-saadisa

السّادِس/السّادِسَة

Seventh
as-saabiᶜ/as-saabiᶜa

السّابِع/السّابِعَة

Fighth
ath-thaamin/ath-thaamina

الثّامِن/الثّامِنَة

Ninth
at-taasiᶜ/at-taasiᶜa

التّاسِع/التّاسِعَة

Tenth
al-ᶜaashir/al-ᶜaashira

العَاشِر/العَاشِرَة

Eleventh
al-Haadee ᶜashar/al-Haadiyta ᶜashara

الحَادِي عَشَر/الحَادِيَة عَشَرَة

Twelfth
ath-thaanee ᶜashar/ath-thaaniyta ᶜashara

الثّاني عَشَر/الثّانِيَة عَشَرَة

Twenty-third
ath-thaalithu wa-al-ᶜishroon/ath-thaalithatu wa-al-ᶜishroon

الثّالثُ والعشرونَ/الثّالثةُ والعشرونَ

Thirty-fourth
ar-raabiᶜu wa-ath-thalaathoon/ar-raabiᶜatu wa-ath-thalaathoon

الرّابِعُ والثلاثونَ/الرّابِعَةُ والثلاثونَ

Fifty-fifth
al-khaamisu wa-al-khaamsoon/al-khaamisatu wa-al-khaamsoon

الخَامِسُ والخمسونَ/الخَامِسَةُ والخمسونَ

EXAMPLES

The first love	al-Hub al-awwal	الحبّ الأوّل
The fifth question	as-su'aal al-khaamis	السؤال الخامس
The sixth article	al-band as-saadis	البند السادس
The eleventh floor	aT-Taabiq al-Haadee'ashar	الطابق الحادي عشر
The third street	ash-shaari' ath-thaalith	الشارع الثالث

VOCABULARY

Phone	haatif/tilifoon	هاتف/تلفون
Street	shaari'	شارع
Number	raqm	رقم
License	rukhSa	رخصة
ID card	biTaaqa (huwiya)	بطاقة (هوية)
Passport	gawaaz safar	جواز سفر
Date	taareekh	تاريخ
Print	Tab'a	طبعة
Profit	ribH	ربح
Page	SafHa	صفحة
Chapter	faSl	فصل
Part (s/p)	guz'/agzaa'	جزء/أجزاء
Copy	nuskha	نسخة

110

Multiple choice: Find the Arabic equivalent to the English numbers.

A. 78956

  I   ٦٥٩٨٧

  II   ٧٨٩٥٦

  III   ٧٨٩٠٦

B. 1002

  I   ٢٠٠١

  II   ١٠٠٢

  III   ٢٥٥١

C. 1st floor

  I   الطابق الأول

  II   الطابق الواحد

  III   الطابق الأولى

D. 2nd house

  I   ٢ بيت

  II   البيت الثاني

  III   البيت الثانية

E. 29/5/2003

  I   ٣٠٠٢/٥ /٢٩

  II   ٢٠٠٣/٥/٩٢

  III   ٢٠٠٣/٥/٢٩

F. 3/2/2102

  I   ٢٠١٢/٢/٣

  II   ٢١٠٢/٢/٣

  III   ٢٠١٢/٣/٢

Translate:

A. Passport Number 2348976

B. 5/11/2009

C. The fifth street

D. Phone no: 1-480-234-4563

TRANSLATE

I. A new author is talking about her first book. Can you figure out how many copies she sold and if she made a profit?

هذه الطبعة الثانية من كتابي الأول. ويتكوّن الكتاب من مئة وعشرين صفحة وينقسم إلى ثلاثة أجزاء وفي كل جزء خمسة فصول وكل فصل من ثماني صفحات. وبيع من هذا الكتاب عشرة آلاف نسخة وبلغ الربح خمسة عشر ألف دولار.

haadhihi aT-Tab^ca ath-thaaniya min kitaabee al-awwal. wa-yatakawwna al-kitaab min mi'a wa-^cishreen SafHa wa-yanqasim ilaa thalaathat agzaa' wa-fee kul guz' khamsat fiSool wa-kul faSl min thamaanee SafaHaat. wa-bee^ca min haadhaa al-kitaab ^cashrat aalaaf nuskha wa-balagha ar-ribH khamsata ^cashar alf doolaar

II. Results are announced for a TV contest. How much did the first place contestant win and what was the third prize?

الجائزة الأولى بقيمة ربع مليون ريال حصل عليها الفائز الأول خالد حسن. والجائزة الثانية بمبلغ مئة ألف ريال حصلت عليها الفائزة الثانية رشا أحمد. أما الجائزة الثالثة وقيمتها خمسون ألف ريال سوف تقسم بين الفائزين الثالث والرابع وسيحصل كل منهما على نصف المبلغ.

al-gaa'iza al-uwlaa bi-qeemat rub^c milyoon rial HaSala ^calyhaa al-faa'iz al-awwal Khaled Hassan. wa-al-gaa'iza ath-thaaniya bi-mablagh mi'at alf rial HaSalt ^calyhaa al-faa'iza ath-thaaniya Rasha Ahmed. amaa al-gaa'iza ath-thaalitha wa-qeematuhaa khamsoon alf rial sawfa tuqqasam bayna al-faai'zayn ath-thaalith wa-ar-raabi^c wa-SayaHSul kul minhumaa ^calaa niSf al-mablagh.

TELLING TIME

To ask the time in Arabic you say:

What is the time please? *kam as-sadʿa min faDlak?*	كَم الساعة مِن فَضلَك؟
It is (the time is) five o'clock *as-sadʿa al-khaamisa*	الساعة الخامسة
Minute/minutes *daqeeqa/daqaaʾiq*	دقيقة/ دقائق
Second/seconds *thaaniya/thawaanin*	ثانية/ثوانٍ

☾ Minutes up to 35 past the hour are added directly to the hour using the conjunction *waaw* (و).

Ten past six *as-sadʿa as-saadisa wa-ʿashar daqaaʾiq*	الساعة السادسة وعشر دقائق

☾ Five to twenty minutes before the hour are expressed by using the word إلّا *(Illaa)* except.

Quarter to five *as-sadʿa al-khaamisa illaa rubʿ*	الساعة الخامسة إلّا الأربع

☾ To specify if it is A.M. or P.M. you say:

Eight o'clock A.M. *as-sadʿa ath-thaamina SabaaHan*	الساعة الثامنة صباحاً
Ten o'clock P.M. *as-sadʿa al-ʿaashira masaaʾn*	الساعة العاشرة مساءً
Twelve noon *as-sadʿa ath-thaaneea ʿashara Zuhran*	الساعة الثانية عشرة ظهراً

113

DAYS OF THE WEEK أيام الأسبوع

Days of the week—except Friday—are derived from numbers. For example, Sunday (الأحد) is derived from number one (واحد) and Monday (الاثنين) has its root in the number two (اثنين).

Sunday	al-aHad	الأحد
Monday	al-ithnayn	الاثنين
Tuesday	ath-thalaathaa'	الثلاثاء
Wednesday	al-arba⸳aa'	الأربعاء
Thursday	al-khamees	الخميس
Friday	al-gum⸳a	الجمعة
Saturday	as-sabt	السبت

☾ When referring to a day of the week, you usually add the word (يوم) before the specific day.

Our meeting is on Sunday	موعدنا يوم الأحد
maw⸳idnaa yawm al-aHad	
See you on Wednesday	أراك يومَ الأربعاء
araaka yawm al-arba⸳aa'	
The wedding is on Thursday	الفرح يوم الخميس
al-faraH yawm al-khamees	
Monday is a holiday	يوم الاثنين إجازة
yawm al-ithnayn igaaza	

114

PARTS OF THE DAY

English	Transliteration	Arabic
Dawn	*fagr*	فجر
Sunrise	*shurook*	شروق
Morning	*SabaaH*	صباح
Noon	*Zuhr*	ظهر
Afternoon	*baᶜd aZ-Zuhr*	بعد الظهر
Sunset	*ghuroob*	غروب
Evening	*masaa´*	مساء
Night	*layl*	ليل
Midnight	*muntaSif al-layl*	منتصف الليل

VOCABULARY

English	Transliteration	Arabic
Hair	*shaᶜr*	شعر
Hairdresser	*muSafaf ash-shaᶜr*	مصفف شعر
Hairdresser	*ⱳuiffeur**	كوافير
Appointment/Date	*mawᶜid*	موعد
Suitable	*munaasib*	مناسب
To cut	*qaSS*	قصّ
Early	*mubakkiran*	مبكّراً
Late	*muta'akhkhiran*	متأخّراً
Store/Shop	*maHall*	محلّ
Holiday/Day off	*igaaza*	إجازة
Month/s	*shahr/shuhoor*	شهر/شهور (أشهر)

* The use of the French equivalent is very common.

115

Five minutes *khams daqaa'iq*	خمس دقائق
Quarter of an hour *rub^c sac^ca*	ربع ساعة
Half an hour *niSf sac^ca*	نصف ساعة
Twenty minutes *thulth sac^ca*	ثلث ساعة
Forty-five minutes *sac^ca illaa rub^c*	ساعة إلاّربع
Forty minutes *sac^ca illaa thulth*	ساعة الاّثلث
One o'clock *as-sac^ca al-waaHida*	الساعة الواحدة
Twelve o'clock *as-sac^ca ath-thaaneea ^cashara*	الساعة الثانية عشرة
Ten past six *as-sac^ca as-saadisa wa-^cashar daqaa'iq*	الساعة السادسة وعشر دقائق
Quarter to five *as-sac^ca al-khaamisa illaa rub^c*	الساعة الخامسة إلاّربع
It is late *al-waqt muta'akhkhiran*	الوقت متأخّراً
It is still early *maa-zaal al-waqt mubakkiran*	مازال الوقت مبكّراً
Early in the morning *fee aS-SabaaH al-baakir*	في الصباح الباكر
One in the afternoon *al-waaHida Zuhran*	الواحدة ظهراً
One after midnight *al-waaHida ba^cd muntaSif al-layl*	الواحدة بعد منتصف الليل
The train came on time *ataa al-qiTaar fee maw^cidh*	أتى القطار في موعده

DIALOGUE

Lina is trying to get an appointment to cut her hair. Follow her conversation with the hairdresser's receptionist.

لينا: أريد موعد لقصّ شعري.

Lina: ureedu maw'id li-qaSS sha'ree

موظّفة الاستقبال: يوجد موعد اليوم الساعة الثانية.

muwaZZafat al-istiqbaal: ywgad maw'id al-yawm as-saa'a ath-thaaniya

لينا: هذا الموعد لايناسبني. ماذا عن غداً؟

Lina: haadhaa al-maw'id la yunaasbnee. maadhaa 'an ghadan?

م. الاستقبال: غداً الاثنين إجازة المحلّ.

M-al-istiqbaal: ghadan al-ithnayn igaazat al-maHall

لينا: أريد موعد في الصباح.

Lina: ureedu maw'id fee aS-SabaaH

م. الاستقبال: يوجد موعد في العاشرة صباحاً يوم الأربعاء.

M-al-istiqbaal: ywgad maw'id fee al-'aashira SabaaHan yawm al-arba'aa'

لينا: لاهذا لايناسبنى. ماذا عن الخميس بعد الظهر؟

Lina: laa haadhaa laa yunaasbnee. maadhaa 'an al-khamees ba'd aZ-Zuhr?

م. الاستقبال: لايوم الخميس سنغلق مبكّراً.

M-al-istiqbaal: laa yawm al khamees su-nughluq mubakkiran

لينا: ماذا عن الأسبوع القادم؟

Lina: maadhaa 'an al-usboo' al-qaadim?

م. الاستقبال: عندي موعد يوم الثلاثاء الساعة الثامنة والنصف.

M-al-istiqbaal: 'indee maw'id yawm ath-thalaathaa' as-saa'a ath-thaamina wa-an-niSf

لينا: الثامنة والنصف مساءً؟

Lina: ath-thaamina wa-an-niSf masaa'n?

م. الاستقبال: لاالثامنة والنصف صباحاً.

M-al-istiqbaal: laa ath-thaamina wa-an-niSf SabaaHan

لينا: حسناً. يوم الثلاثاء ١٨ نوفمبر الساعة الثامنة والربع صباحاً.

Lina: Hasanan yawm ath-thalaathaa' 18 noovembir as-saa'a ath-thaamina wa-ar-rub' SabaaHan

م. الاستقبال: لاالثامنة والنصف.

M-al-istiqbaal: laa ath-thaamina wa-an-niSf

Write down the time shown on the clocks.

١ أستيقظ من النوم في الساعة----
I wake up at----

١١ أذهب إلى عملي في الساعة----
I go to work at----

١١١ أعود إلى البيت في الساعة----
I return home at----

IV أخرج إلى العشاء في الساعة----
I go out for dinner at----

V أذهب إلى النوم في الساعة----
I go to bed at----

Months

Western Calendar

In Arabic, the names of the months are written in two different ways. The first is derived from the Georgian calendar; the other is used in the Eastern Middle Eastern countries (Syria, Lebanon, Jordan, and Iraq).

	EASTERN	GEORGIAN
January	كانون الثاني *kaanoon ath-thaanee*	يناير *yanaayir*
February	شباط *shubaaT*	فبراير *fabraayir*
March	آذار *aadhaar*	مارس *maaris*
April	نيسان *naysaan*	أبريل *abreel*
May	أيّار *ayyaar*	مايو *maayoo*
June	حزيران *Hazyraan*	يونيو *yooniyoo*
July	تمّوز *tammooz*	يوليو *yooliyoo*
August	آب *aab*	أغسطس *aghusTus*
September	أيلول *aylool*	سبتمبر *sibtambir*
October	تشرين الأوّل *tishreen al-awwal*	أكتوبر *uctoobir*
November	تشرين الثّاني *tishreen ath-thaanee*	نوفمبر *noovembir*
December	كانون الأوّل *kaanoon al-awwal*	ديسمبر *deesambir*

119

Months-Islamic Calendar

The Islamic calendar is a lunar calendar that has 12 lunar months, each month is either 29 or 30 days. The beginning of the month is determined by the birth of the moon (when the crescent first appears). A lunar year is 11 days shorter than the solar year, that is why Islamic months do not correspond to the Western solar ones. The Islamic calendar is also called the Hijree (root word هجر to emigrate) since it marks the date when the prophet Mohammed emigrated from Mecca to Medina in the year 622 A.D. The year 2008, for example, corresponds to the Islamic year 1428/1429.

muHarram	محرّم
Safar	صفر
rabee al-awwal*	ربيع الأوّل
rabee al-aakhar (ath-thaanee)*	ربيع الآخر (الثاني)
jumaadaa al-uwlaa	جمادى الأولى
jumaadaa al-aakhira (ath-thaaneea)	جمادى الآخرة (الثانية)
rajab	رجب
*sha*baan*	شعبان
ramadaan	رمضان
shawwaal	شوّال
*dhoo al-qa*da*	ذو القعدة
dhoo al-Hijja	ذو الحجّة

An alternative way of saying the Arabic months is included within brackets.

ⓒ In Arabic, the Western calendar is known as السّنة الميلاديّة (from the word ميلاد or birth) and uses the letter م as an abbreviation. The Islamic calendar uses the letter ه as an abbreviation for السّنة الهجريّة. In English, it is abbreviated A.H. from the Latin word *Anno Hegirae.*

Examples

Year 2009 A.D.   سنة ٢٠٠٩ م

Year 1431 A.H.   سنة ١٤٣١ ه

In most Arabic publications and correspondence, both dates are written.

عام ١٤٢٠ ه الموافق ١٩٩٩ م

Year 1420 A.H. (hijree) corresponding to 1999 A.D.

٧ يونيو ٢٠٠٧م – ٢١ جمادى الأولى ١٤٢٨ه

7 June 2007 A.D.– 21 jumaadaa al-uwlaa 1428 A.H.

Seasons   فصول السّنة

Season is *faSl* (فصل) in Arabic. When referring to seasons, the definite article is used.

Spring	*ar-rabee*ᶜ	الرّبيع
Summer	*aS-Sayf*	الصّيف
Autumn	*al-khareef*	الخريف
Winter	*ash-shitaa'*	الشّتاء

121

VOCABULARY

Travel and weather

Weather	Taqs	طَقس
Heat	Harra	حَرّ
Cold	bard	برد
Rain	maTar	مَطر
Cloud/s	saHaab/suHub	سحاب/سحب
Fog	Dabaab	ضَباب
Beach	shaaTi'	شاطئ
Sea/s	baHr/biHaar	بحر/بحار
Sand	rimaal	رمال
Snow	thalg	ثلج
Ice	galeed	جليد
Air	hawaa'	هواء
Storm	ᶜaaSifa	عاصفة
Holiday	igaaza	إجازة
Trip	riHla	رحلة
Ticket	tadhkara	تذكرة
Airport	maTaar	مطار
Aeroplane	Taa'ira	طائرة
Station	maHaTTa	محطّة
Train	qiTaar	قطار
Bus	autoobees	أتوبيس
Reservation	Hagz	حجز
To become crazy (crazy)	ganna (magnoon)	جنَّ (مجنون)

122

Ahmed and his friends are discussing what they will do on their summer vacation.

أحمد: ماذا ستفعلون في إجازة الصيف؟

Ahmed: maadhaa sa-tafʿaloona fee igaazat aS-Sayf?

هدى: أنا لا أحبّ الحرّ وسوف أمضي شهور الصيف في الساحل الشمالي.

Hoda: anaa laa uHibu al-Harr wa-sawfa amDee shuhoor aS-Sayf fee as-saaHil ash-shamaalee,

ماهر: أنا لا أكرهه الحرّ وسوف أبقى في المدينة طوال شهري يوليو وأغسطس.

Maher: anaa laa akrahu al-Harr wa-sawfa abqaa fee al-madeena Tiwaal shahree yooliyoo wa-aghusTus.

أحمد: لدي الكثير من الأعمال هذا الصيف وفي الشتاء سوف أذهب لزيارة أخي في كندا.

Ahmed: laday al-katheer min al-aʿmaal haadhaa aS-Sayf wa-fee ash-shitaa' sawfa adhhabu li-zyaarat akhee fee canadaa

ماهر: كندا في ديسمبر! هل جننت؟

Maher: canadaa fee deesambir! hal ganantu?

أحمد: أنا لا أكرهه البرد وأحبّ أن أرى الثلج.

Ahmed: anaa laa akrahu al-bard wa-uHibu an araa ath-thalg.

هدى: أنا لا أحتمل البرد ومن الممكن أن أشاهد الثلج في التلفزيون وأنا أستمتع بالشاطئ.

Hoda: anaa laa aHtamilu al-bard wa-min al-mumkin an ushaahid ath-tahlg fee at-tiliviзyoon wa-anaa astamtaʿu bi-ash-shaaTi'.

123

EXERCISE 1

Tarek and Dina are getting married and have sent out their wedding invitations to their friends and family. Can you translate this invitation?

مهندس حسن أحمد وحرمه
رجل الأعمال زياد محمد وحرمه
يتشرفان بدعوتكم لحضور حفل زفاف

طارق حسن على دينا زياد

وذلك يوم الخميس ٩ يوليو/ تموز عام ٢٠٠٨م الموافق ٥ رجب١٤٢٩هـ
سيقام الحفل الساعة السابعة مساءً في قاعة الاحتفالات بفندق برج العرب

نتمنى لاطفالكم نوماً هانئاً

EXERCISE 2

Fill in the blank.

١   موعدنا يوم --- ١١ ------
1. Our appointment is on Monday, 11 December

١١   تأجل الاجتماع لشهر ------
2. The meeting was postponed to July

١١١   المحل مغلق يوم ------
3. The shop is closed on Sunday

١٧   يصوم المسلمون في شهر -------
4. Muslims fast during Ramadan

124

Using an Arabic Dictionary

There are two major types of Arabic dictionaries: one that lists entries alphabetically and another that lists entries according to their root.

Entries listed alphabetically are easier to use. To gain proficiency in the Arabic language, however, you must be able to locate words according to their root.

Arabic words are derived from three—in rare occasions four—consonants known as root letters. When looking up an Arabic word, you first need to identify its root. Once you have found it, you will find all other words derived from the same root.

For example: To check the word تذكار (*tadhkaar*) in a dictionary that lists entries alphabetically, you will find it under the letter (ت). To check the word المذكّرات (*al-mudhakkaraat*), you will have to omit the prefix *alif laam* (ال) and check the word under the letter (م).

To check these same two words in a traditional Arabic dictionary, you will first need to locate the root word. In this case, the root is ذَكَر (*dhakara*), to remember. Once you have found the root verb, you will find the derived verbs and all other words sharing the same root.

Examples

To remember	*dhakara*	ذكر
To study	*dhaakar*	ذاكر
To know by heart	*istadhkar*	إستذكر

The same root is also the core of many other words. These words are usually related to the general idea or meaning behind the root.

EXAMPLES

Notebook	mudhakkira	مُذَكِّرة
Memoirs	mudhakkiraat	مُذَكِّرات
Memory	dhaakira	ذاكِرة
Memento/Souvenir	tadhkaar	تَذكار

Here are some tips to help you find the root letters of a word.

☾ Omit the indefinite article *alif laam* (الـ) and any attached prepositions, possessive suffixes, the feminine mark, or any other prefix or suffix you recognize.

☾ If you recognize that a verb is in either the present or the imperative, change it to the past tense and conjugate the verb in the third person masculine singular (he).

☾ If it is a derived verb—meaning that the stem has been modified by the addition of one, two, or three letters—it should be returned to its stem form. To help you do this, remember that the root word should rhyme with *faᶜla* (فعل) or Form I of the verb (see *al-mizan aS-Sarfee* on page 135).

☾ Finding the right root may take some trial and error. The greatest advantage is that once you locate the root word, you will find all other words associated with it. This is an excellent practice to enrich your vocabulary.

127

Consider the root word ᶜalama (عَلِم), which means "to know." Once you locate the root, you will be able to check all of these entries.

To teach	ᶜallama	عَلَّمَ
To inform	aᶜlama	أعلَمَ
To inquire	istaᶜlama	استعلَمَ
Educated	mutaᶜallim	مُتَعَلِّم
Teacher	muᶜallim/muᶜallima	مُعَلِّم/مُعَلِّمة
Information	istiᶜlaamaat	استعلامات
Media	iᶜlaam	إعلام
Instructions	taᶜleemaat	تَعليمات
Information office	maktab al-istiᶜlaamaat	مَكتَب الاستعلامات

EXAMPLES

Few Arabic words have a root of four letters

To shake (root)	zalzala	زَلزَلَ
Earthquake	zalzaal	زلزال
To awaken doubts (root)	waswasa	وَسوَسَ
Misgiving/Suspicion	waswasa	وسوسة
Obsessed with delusions	muwaswas	موسوس
To embellish (root)	zakhrafa	زَخرَفَ
Decoration/Ornament	zakhaarif	زخارف
To scatter (root)	baᶜthara	بَعثَرَ
Scattered	mubaᶜthar	مُبَعثَر

In order to find the meaning of these words in a dictionary, you need to find the root word. Cross out these words to find the root.

ت	ا	ر	ا	ط	م
ط	ر	ي	ط	ن	ط
ة	ر	ئ	ا	ط	ي
ر	ا	ي	ط	ي	و
ر	ر	ئ	ا	ط	ر

مطارات
طائر
طيار
طائرة
نطير
طيور

Under which root would these words appear in a dictionary?

I شهود

II السلام

III فرحان

IV تفتحت

V أفكار

VI مستشفيات

Irregular Verbs

Verbs Beginning with a Weak Letter

Let's look at the verb وَعَدَ (to promise):

	Imperative	Present	Past	
I		أَعِدُ	وعدتُ	أنا
You (m)	عِد	تَعِدُ	وعدتَ	أنتَ
You (f)	عِدي	تَعِدينَ	وعدتِ	أنتِ
He		يَعِدُ	وعدَ	هُوَ
She		تَعِدُ	وعدتْ	هيَ
We		نَعِدُ	وعدنا	نحنُ
You (m,p)	عِدوا	تَعِدونَ	وعدتُم	أنتُم
You (f,p)	عِدنَ	تَعِدنَ	وعدتنَّ	أنتُنَّ
They (m)		يَعِدونَ	وعدوا	هُم
They (f)		يَعِدنَ	وعدنَ	هُنَّ
You (m,d) (f,d)	عِدا	تَعِدانِ	وعدتما	أنتُما
They (m,d)		يَعِدانِ	وعدا	هُمَا
They (f,d)		تَعِدانِ	وعدتا	هُمَا

Verbs with a Weak Letter in the Middle

Let's look at the verb قالَ (to say):

	IMPERATIVE	PRESENT	PAST	
I		أقولُ	قلتُ	أنا
You (m)	قلْ	تقولُ	قلتَ	أنتَ
You (f)	قولي	تقولينَ	قلتِ	أنتِ
He		يقولُ	قالَ	هُوَ
She		تقولُ	قالتْ	هيَ
We		نقولُ	قلنا	نحنُ
You (m,p)	قولوا	تقولونَ	قلتم	أنتُم
You (f,p)	قلنَ	تقلنَ	قلتنّ	أنتنّ
They (m)		يقولونَ	قالوا	هُم
They (f)		يقلنَ	قلنَ	هُنّ
You (m,d) (f,d)	قولا	تقولانِ	قلتما	أنتُما
They (m,d)		يقولانِ	قالا	هُمَا
They (f,d)		تقولانِ	قالتا	هُمَا

131

VERBS WITH A WEAK LETTER IN THE MIDDLE

Let's look at another verb with a weak letter in the middle of its root, the verb كَانَ (to be/exist):

	IMPERATIVE	PRESENT	PAST	
I		أكونُ	كنتُ	أنا
You (m)	كُنْ	تكونُ	كنتَ	أنتَ
You (f)	كُونِي	تكونينَ	كنتِ	أنتِ
He		يكونُ	كانَ	هُوَ
She		تكونُ	كانتْ	هِيَ
We		نكونُ	كنا	نحنُ
You (m,p)	كُونُوا	تكونونَ	كنتم	أنتُم
You (f,p)	كُنَّ	تكنَّ	كنتنَّ	أنتُنَّ
They (m)		يكونونَ	كانوا	هُم
They (f)		يكنَّ	كنَّ	هُنَّ
You (m,d) (f,d)	كُونا	تكونانِ	كنتما	أنتُما
They (m,d)		يكونانِ	كانا	هُمَا
They (f,d)		تكونانِ	كانتا	هُمَا

132

VERB WITH A FINAL WEAK LETTER

Let's look at the verb رمى (to throw):

	IMPERATIVE	PRESENT	PAST	
I		ارمي	رميتُ	أنا
You (m)	اِرمِ	ترمي	رميتَ	أنتَ
You (f)	اِرمي	تَرمين	رميتِ	أنتِ
He		يرمي	رمى	هُوَ
She		ترمي	رمت	هيَ
We		نرمي	رمينا	نحنُ
You (m,p)	اِرموا	ترمونَ	رميتم	أنتُم
You (f,p)	اِرمينَ	تَرمينْ	رميتن	أنتنَّ
They (m)		يرمونَ	رموا	هُم
They (f)		يرمينْ	رمينَ	هُنَّ
You (m,d) (f,d)	اِرمِيا	ترميان	رَمَيتُما	أنتُما
They (m,d)		يرميانِ	رَمَيا	هُمَا
They (f,d)		ترميانِ	رَمَتا	هُمَا

DOUBLED VERBS

Let's look at the verb كَفَّ (to refrain/stop):

	IMPERATIVE	PRESENT	PAST	
I		أكفُ	كففتُ	أنا
You (m)	كفَّ	تكفُ	كففتَ	أنتَ
You (f)	كفّي	تكفّينَ	كففتِ	أنتِ
He		يكفُ	كفَّ	هُوَ
She		تكفُ	كفَّت	هِيَ
We		نكفُ	كففنا	نحنُ
You (m,p)	كفّوا	تكفّونَ	كففتم	أنتُم
You (f,p)	أكففنَ	تكففنَ	كففتنَّ	أنتُنَّ
They (m)		يكفّونَ	كفّوا	هُم
They (f)		يكففنَ	كففنَ	هُنَّ
You (m,d) (f,d)	كفّا	تكفّانِ	كففتما	أنتُما
They (m,d)		يكفّانِ	كفّا	هُمَا
They (f,d)		تكفّانِ	كفّتا	هُمَا

134

THE TEN PATTERNS OF VERBS
KNOWN AS AL-MIZAN AS-SARFEE

الميزان الصرفي

From the root of a verb, other verbs can be derived. In theory up to nine different forms can be derived from one root. These verbs are formed by adding, one, two or three letters to the root verb. In Arabic, linguists use the root فعل as a pattern. Any derived verb should follow one of the ten patterns provided. In Arabic–English dictionaries, derived verbs are given the Roman numerals I–X, where I is the root verb.

THE TEN PATTERNS OF VERBS (الميزان الصرفي)

FORM I	فَعَلَ
FORM II	فَعَّلَ
FORM III	فَاعَلَ
FORM IV	أفعَلَ
FORM V	تَفَعَّلَ
FORM VI	تَفَاعَلَ
FORM VII	انفَعَلَ
FORM VIII	افتَعَلَ
FORM IX	افعَلَّ
FORM X	استَفعَلَ

135

Answers to Exercises

Part I: Pronouns

Translation, Dialogue, page 14
(translation is given word for word)

Mona: Good Morning.
Tarek: Good Morning. I am Tarek.
Mona: Hello I am Mona. And who are they?
Tarek: They are my friends. They don't speak Arabic.
Mona: Where are they from?
Tarek: He is from Canada and they (d) are from America.
Mona: And where are you from?
Tarek: I am from Cairo.
Mona: Hello and Welcome. Please come in.
Tarek: Thank you.

Exercise, page 15

A - iv; B - i; C - ii; D - iii; E - vi; F- v

Puzzle, page 15

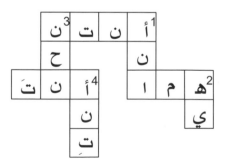

Attached Pronouns

Puzzle, page 18

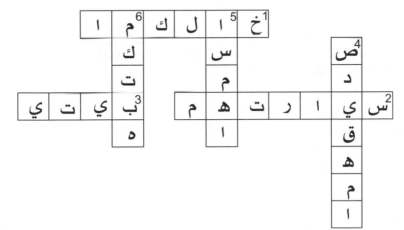

Demonstrative

Exercise, page 22

ا هذا أخي

II هذان أخي وأختي

III هذه عائلتي

IV هؤلاء أصدقائي

V هنا بيتي

VI وهناك مدرستي

Mona: Your house is beautiful.
Hala: This is our house, mine and my family's.
Mona: Where is your room?
Hala: This is my room, and this is my brother's room.
Mona: His room is large, and these are his pictures?
Hala: No. These are my sister's pictures. These are her friends.
Mona: And this is your car.
Hala: Yes. This is our car.

Receptionist: Welcome to our hotel.
Youssef: Thank you. Where is the restaurant, please?
Receptionist: Here is the restaurant, and there is the garden and the swimming pool.
Youssef: And this is my room?
Receptionist: No this is the manager's office. This is your room. Please come in.
Youssef: Thank you.
Receptionist: Here is the bedroom and there is the bathroom. This is the hotel's guide. This is a small fridge. That is the balcony and these are two keys for the room. I wish you a pleasant stay.

Part II: Nouns & Adjectives
Translation, Dialogue, page 40

Waiter: Here are glasses, plates, and clean napkins.
Rania: This glass is not clean.
Hend: And this plate is also not clean. And I want a new napkin.
Waiter: Here are knives and forks.
Noha: Please change this knife, and I want a spoon.
Waiter: I will bring you spoons and fresh juices.
Hend: I asked for an apple not apple juice.
Rania and Noha: And we asked for two glasses of milk, not juice.
Waiter: Here are the eggs, the sandwich, and loaves of bread.
Rania: What's all of this? I want a loaf and an egg.
Noha: And I want sandwiches, not a sandwich.
Waiter: Here is the bill, or would you want separate bills?
Rania: No, one bill. Thank you.
Waiter: You are welcome. You are a good customer. I wish all customers were like you!

Exercise, page 41

1- iii ; 2- i ; 3- i; 4- iii; 5- i

Exercise, page 42

A		B		C	
‎ا	أنوار	‎ا	عقول	‎ا	جبال
‎اا	أشجار	‎اا	نمور	‎اا	بحار
‎ااا	أطفال	‎ااا	أسود	‎ااا	رياح
				‎اٰٰ	سهام

D
ا خرائط
اا حدائق
ااا زبائن

A- iii; B- iii; C- ii; D- i

١ الرجل الوسيم

١١ حقيبة سوداء

١١١ السلام العادل

١٧ أفكار جديدة

٧ قصة جيدة

٧١ الطفلة الشقية

A famous director is looking for talented actors:

الزوج الخائن:
شعر أسود
قامة طويلة
عضلات قوية
عينان جذابتان

الزوجة المهملة:
قامة قصيرة
جسم بدين
صوت عال
عينان ضيقتان

العشيقة الجميلة:
قامة رشيقة
شعر أشقر
عينان واسعتان
صوت ناعم

Part iii: Verbs

I   We met yesterday
II   We married last year
III   She went to visit her friend*
IV   You (m,p) missed a golden opportunity
V   He got a raise
VI   They (f,p) laughed a lot
VII   They (d) wrote their marriage contract
VIII   You (f,p) listened to the new song
IX   They (m,d) drank coffee
X   She drew a beautiful painting*
XI   I played in the garden *

*She and I have the same prefix ending but different vowel marks.
The final taa' associated with "she" does not take a vowel, while the
one associated with "I" takes a Damma. Verbs associated with "You"
masculine and feminine singular also have the same prefix as "She and
I" but different vowel marks see page 54.

Exercise, page 63

I   They (f,p)
II   He
III   He
IV   She
V   We
VI   I
VII   She
VIII   They (m,p)
IX   She
X   I
XI   She or You (m,s)
XII   We
XIII   I

هو جلس في المطعم أمس	I
نحن سوف نذهب إلى المسرح غداً	II
هي تتحدث معه الآن	III
هم ينتظرون منذ الصباح	IV
هن ينجحن دائماً	V
هما يضحكان كثيراً	VI

هم يلعبون الكرة هم لعبوا الكرة العبوا الكرة	II

They (m) play the ball.
They played the ball.
Play the ball.

تتحدث أختي تحدثت أختي تحدثي	III

My sister is speaking.
My sister spoke.
Speak.

يفتح أحمد الباب فتح أحمد الباب افتح الباب	IV

Ahmed is opening the door.
Ahmed opened the door.
Open the door.

هن يذهبنَ إلى السوق هن ذهبنَّ إلى السوق اذهبنَ إلى السوق	V

They (f) go to the market.
They went to the market.
Go to the market.

العروسان يكتبان الكتاب العروسان كتبا الكتاب أكتبا الكتاب	VI

The bride and groom are writing their marriage contract.
The bride and groom wrote their marriage contract.
Write your marriage contract.

142

Nabil: Where shall we go today?
Sameh: I want to go out and forget what happened to me yesterday.
Nabil: What happened yesterday?
Sameh: I woke up late. I was in a hurry and by mistake, I wore a black shoe and a brown one. And I drove my car too fast and I almost hit a man and his wife, and they quarrelled with me. Then a policeman stopped me and he gave me a ticket, and I arrived late to work.
Nabil: And what did your colleagues do?
Sameh: They quarrelled with me. And I forgot an appointment with the company's most important client. And they were not pleased with my work. And also my boss, she was not pleased with my work.
Nabil: And after this?
Sameh: I forgot my appointment with my fiancée and she quarrelled with me.
Nabil. I know a very good place for your condition. Let's go.

EXERCISE, PAGE 75

IV تفهّم	III أشرك	II أخرج	I سلَم
أفهم	اشترك	تخرج	سالم
تفاهم	شارك	استخرج	استسلم
استفهم			

VII تحسب	VI استقطع	V تفتح
حاسب	قاطع	فاتح
		استفتح

143

عزيزي أبي

أنا أعلم أني لم أكتب إليك منذ فترة طويلة. أنا سمعت أنك حصلت على ربح وفير من عملك. أنا أبعث إليك بأرق تحية واصدقائي أيضاً يبعثون إليك بتحيتهم. نحن نريد أن ناتي لنراك ولكن ليس لدينا سيارة جديدة. وفي النهاية أنا أعلم أنك سوف تتذكر عيد ميلادي.

مع خالص التحية
أبنك المخلص

طارق

TRANSLATION

Dear father,

I know that I did not write to you in a long time. I heard that you received an abundant profit from your work. I send you my best regards. My friends also send their best regards. We want to come to see you but we do not have a new car. Finally, I know that you will remember my birthday.

Your faithful son,
Tarek

كفوا عن الخناق واشربوا اللبن ثم اغسلوا وجوهكم. منى وريم اذهبا إلى غرفتكما وأحمد اخلع ملابسك. والآن ناموا. لاانتظروا اعطوني قبلة ثم اذهبوا إلى النوم.

TRANSLATION

Stop fighting and drink the milk, then wash your faces. Mona and Reem go to your room, and Ahmed take off your clothes. And now sleep. No, wait. Give me a kiss and then go to sleep.

EXERCISE, MULTIPLE CHOICE, PAGE 79

i-A ; ii-B ; iii- B; iv- C; v-B; vi-C

PART IV: QUESTIONS, PREPOSITIONS & NEGATION

EXERCISE, PAGE 85

أين أنت؟	I
من هي؟	II
كيف حالك؟	III
أين السيارة؟	IV
هل لديكم غرفة؟	V
من تتحدث؟	VI
كم تكسب في اليوم؟	VII
مااسمك؟	VIII
أين المطعم؟	IX
في أية ساعة تستيقظ؟	X
كم ثمن هذا الخاتم؟	XI
هل يمكن أن تعيد السؤال؟	XII
متى أتيت وأين تمكث؟	XIII

Journalist 1: What happened?
Police Inspector: A thief has raided the museum.
Journalist 2: When did the theft occur?
Police Inspector: Yesterday evening.
Journalist 3: At what time?
Police Inspector: After midnight.
Journalist 4: Did you catch the thief?
Police Inspector: Yes.
Journalist 4: What is his description?
Police Inspector: A short and very fat young man.
Journalist 1: Was anything stolen from the museum?
Police Inspector: Yes, a precious antique statue.
Journalist 3: How much is this statue worth?
Police Inspector: Priceless.
Journalist 4: Did you find the statue?
Police Inspector: No. Not yet.
Journalist 1: How did the thief raid the museum?
Police Inspector: He jumped from a small window.
Journalist 3: And how did a very fat man jump in from a small window?
Police Inspector: He had a partner.
Journalist 4: And who is this partner?
Police Inspector: Ah, Ah, Ah,... a monkey.
Journalist 2: A monkey! And did you catch the monkey?
Police Inspector: No, not yet.

Exercise 1, page 91

اذهب إلى غرفتك وابحث عن مفتاح الدولاب وبالدولاب
يوجد رفّ وعلى الرفّ يوجد صندوق وفي الصندوق
توجد النظارة. سامي أنت تنسى دائماً كأبيك!

Sami go to your room and look for the closet's key. In the closet, there is a shelf, and on this shelf there is a box, and in the box, are the glasses. Sami you always forget, just like your father!

ا   أقيم مع أصدقائي

II   هي من أمريكا

III   لن أعلق على هذا السؤال

IV   ذاكر لتنجح

V   يجب أن أتحدث مع سارة

VI   حدثني عن أحمد

VII   هي تقود بسرعة جنونية

VIII   لا أحب الذهاب إلى العمل

دكتور: ماذا بك؟

يوسّف: عندي ألم في جسمي وصداع في رأسي.

دكتور: ولكَ على هذا الحال فترة طويلة؟

يوسّف: لي على هذا الحال أسبوع.

دكتور: تفضل على السرير. اِسترح عليه.

(بعد الكشف)

دكتور: عندكَ حمّى عليكَ بالراحة التّامة.

يوسّف: هل أحتاج إلى دواء؟

دكتور: نعم. تفضّل هذا الدواء فيه الشفاء بإذن الله.

يوسّف: شكراً يادكتور سعدتُ بلقاءك.

147

Doctor: What is wrong with you (what is with you)?
Youssef: I have pain in my body, and a headache.
Doctor: And you have been in this condition for a long time?
Youssef: I have been in this condition for a week.
Doctor: Get on the bed. Rest on it.
After Examination
Doctor: You have a fever. You have to rest completely.
Youssef: Do I need medicine?
Doctor: Yes. Take this medicine. God willing, this medicine will
cure you (there will be a cure in it).
Youssef: Thank you, doctor. Pleased to meet you.

EXERCISE **1**, PAGE **99**

لا أعرف ماذا أرتدي اليوم. لن أرتدي الفستان الأزرق انه ضيق
والفستان الأحمر لم أعد أحبه اما الفستان الأخضر لم يعد
يناسبني. والفستان الأصفر واسع جداً. ولن أرتدي الأسود
انا ماأحببت الأسود ابداً. لايوجد شئ آخر أرتديه. حسناً
لايوجد حل غير ان أذهب إلى التسوق ولكن ماذا أرتدي الآن!

TRANSLATION, PAGE **99**

I do not know what to wear today. I will not wear the blue dress,
it is tight. And the red dress, I do not like it anymore. And
about the green dress, it does not suit me anymore. And the
yellow dress is too wide. And I won't wear the black dress, I
have never liked black. There is nothing left to wear. Fine,
there is no solution but to go shopping. But what should I wear
now!

لن أذهب إلى السينما   I

ماسمعت آخر الأخبار   II
لم أسمع آخر الأخبار

لاأفهم الدرس   III

لن أسافر غداً إلى المغرب   IV

لاأتحدث العربية   V

ماخرجت مع منى مساء أمس   VI
لم أخرج مع منى مساء أمس

PART V: NUMBERS, TIME, DAYS & MONTHS

MULTIPLE CHOICE, PAGE *111*

A - ii; B- ii ; C-i ; D -ii ; E- iii ; F-ii

TRANSLATION, PAGE *111*

جواز سفر رقم ٢٣٤٨٩٧٦   I

٢٠٠٩/١١/٥   II

الشارع الخامس   III

تليفون رقم: ٤٥٦٣-٢٣٤-٤٨٠-١   IV

TRANSLATION, PAGE *112*

New author talking about her book:

This is the second edition of my first book. The book consists of one hundred and twenty pages and is divided into three parts. In each part, there are five chapters, and each chapter has eight pages. The book sold ten thousand copies, with a fifteen thousand dollar profit.

149

Translation, page 112
Prize winners:

The first prize, for the amount of one quarter million Riyal, went to the first winner Khaled Hassan. The second prize, for the amount of one hundred thousand Riyal, was won by the second prize winner, Rasha Ahmed. And the third prize, for the amount of fifty thousand Riyal, will be divided between the third and fourth winners. Each will receive half the amount.

Translation, Dialogue, page 117

Lina: I want an appointment to cut my hair.
Receptionist: There is an appointment available today at two o'clock
Lina: No, this appointment does not suit me. What about tomorrow?
Receptionist: Tomorrow is Monday, the shop's day off.
Lina: I want a morning appointment.
Receptionist: There is an appointment available at ten o'clock a.m. on Wednesday.
Lina: No, this does not suit me. What about Thursday afternoon?
Receptionist: No, on Thursday we will close early.
Lina: What about next week?
Receptionist: I have an appointment available on Tuesday at eight thirty.
Lina: Eight thirty in the evening?
Receptionist: No, eight thirty in the morning.
Lina. Fine. Tuesday, 18th November, at quarter past eight in the morning
Receptionist: No, half past eight.

ا   الساعة السادسة إلا عشر دقائق

II   الساعة الثامنة وعشرون دقيقة

III   الساعة الخامسة وعشر دقائق

IV   الساعة السابعة والنصف

V   الساعة التاسعة

TRANSLATION: DIALOGUE, PAGE *123*

Ahmed: What will you do in the summer vacation?
Hoda: I do not like the heat, and will spend the summer months in the northern coast.
Maher: I do not hate the heat and will stay in the city for the months of July and August.
Ahmed: I have lots of work this summer, and in the winter I will go to visit my brother in Canada.
Maher: Canada in December! Are you crazy?
Ahmed: I do not hate the cold, and I would like to see the snow.
Hoda: I cannot stand the cold, and I can watch the snow on television while I enjoy the beach.

TRANSLATION, PAGE *124*

Engineer & Mrs Hassan Ahmed
Businessman & Mrs Ziad Mohamed
Have the honour to invite you to the wedding of

Tarek Hassan & Dina Ziad

On Thursday July 9, 2008 corresponding to 5 Rajab 1529 A. H. The reception will be held at seven o'clock at the banquet hall at Bourg al-Arab hotel

We wish your children sweet dreams.

151

FILL IN THE BLANK, PAGE 124

ا موعدنا يوم الاثنين ١١ ديسمبر

II تأجل الاجتماع لشهر يوليو

III المحل مغلق يوم الأحد

IV يصوم المسلمون في شهر رمضان

EXERCISE 1, PAGE 129

The missing word:

طير (طار)*

* *In dictionaries, the stem of the verb is given in the perfect or the past tense. The verb in the present is given between brackets.*

EXERCISE 2, PAGE 129

ا شهد

II سلم

III فرح

IV فتح

V فكر

VI شفى

Index

153